A New Moment in the Americas

Edited by
Robert S. Leiken

Transaction Publishers
New Brunswick (U.S.A.) and London (U.K.)

**Cataloging-in-Publication Data
on file in the Library of Congress**

ISBN-1-56000-811-3
Printed in the United States of America
00 99 98 97 96 95 94   8 7 6 5 4 3 2 1

Contents

Preface and Acknowledgments

In the late summer of 1994, with December's Summit of the Americas on the horizon, a planning committee began to explore the possibility of holding a meeting, an "encuentro," of cultural leaders from around the hemisphere in advance of the Summit. One objective was to show the rich historical and cultural context in which the Summit would unfold.

The response to our inquiries was overwhelming. "You're on the mark," we heard from all corners of the hemisphere. "There is indeed what you're calling 'A New Moment in the Americas.' How can we help?"

The dual enterprise of organizing a meeting and a book to commemorate this new moment in a few hectic weeks could not have been achieved without assistance from many quarters.

This project simply would not have been possible without the creative thinking and support of Penn Kemble, deputy director of the United States Information Agency, and the daily, no, hourly miracles performed by my talented and tolerant associates Randy Wells and Gina Marie Lichacz. And those miracles were performed six or seven days a week, ten or twelve hours a day, for more than two months. Gina Marie was in charge of handling the editing and translating and coordinating all the other elements involved in rapidly publishing a volume in two languages; Randy with virtually everything else, from invitations, communications, and press relations to making computers work. And the administrative support and cross-cultural skills of our assistant, Paulina Hines, made her a vital player on our team.

The Planning Committee deserves special thanks for their key role, including Ambassador Ambler H. Moss, Jr., director of the North-South Center; Georgette Dorn of the Library of Congress; Peter Hakim, president of the Inter-American Dialogue; Adrian Karatnycky, president of Freedom House; Lillian Pubillones of the National Endowment for Democracy; Mark Falcoff of the American Enterprise Institute; Dolores Martin of the Library of Congress; John Dwyer of USIA; and Beatrice Rangel Mantilla from Venezuela. I trust the other members of the Committee will not object if I single out Mr. Falcoff, Ms. Martin, Mr. Dwyer, and Ms. Rangel for their assistance beyond the call of duty.

I also want to thank the members of our Advisory Committee: German Arciniegas from Colombia, Elena Castedo from the United States, Fernando Cepeda from Colombia, Gustavo Gorriti from Peru, Sir Alister McIntyre from Jamaica, Morton Abramowitz of the Carnegie Endowment for International Peace, Jean Bethke Elshtain of Vanderbilt University, Todd Gitlin of the University of California at Berkeley, Orlando Patterson of Harvard University, and Michael Novak of the American Enterprise Institute. Again let me give special thanks to Elena Castedo and Jean Elshtain for their advice and recommendations.

In order to bring off a conversation which would be both lively and congenial, we consulted individuals familiar with the various worlds (academic, cultural, and hemispheric) represented there. Those who provided important advice included Edgardo Krebs, Viron P. Vaky, Malcom Deas, William D. Rodgers, Abe Lowenthal, Devon Gaffney, Steven Blank, Susan Kaufman Purcell, Saul Sosnowski, Bernard Aronson, Marta Patricia Baltodano, Adam Meyerson, Ralph Chambers, Horacio Crespo, David Asman, Glen Hartley, Robert Putnam, Steven and Abby Thernstrom, Rick Hertzberg, Alex Star, Robert Silvers and Melanie Thernstrom.

We are thankful for the encouragement from U.S. government officials, including Director of USIA Joseph D. Duffey; Special Advisor to the Policy and Planning Staff of the Department of State Luigi Einaudi; Assistant Secretary of State Alexander Watson; Deputy Assistant Secretary of State Arturo Valenzuela; Vice President Al Gore; and especially Senior Director for Inter-American Affairs at the National Security Council Richard Feinberg.

A special thanks to Robin Rosenberg of the North-South Center for interrupting many meetings to deal with crises, Stanley Crouch for arranging our spectacular musical evening, and Judy Watson for her helpful ideas on protocol.

At USIA, Lauren Monsen provided initial assistance, Sue Walitsky handled the enormous task of travel and logistics for the meeting, and Gil Callaway was our friendly troubleshooter.

Those who helped with copy editing, proofreading, translating, transcribing, and fact-checking included Elizabeth Schoenfeld, Vicente Echerri, Roberto Tejada, Erick Bridoux, Ana Alonso Coyne, Richard Boyd, Santiago Malave, and Richard Downes of the North-South Center as well as the entire North-South Center Editorial and Publications Staff, including especially Kathleen Hamman, Mary Mapes, and Cynthia Jenney.

The funding for the meeting and the publication was provided mainly by matching grants from the United States Information Agency and the North-South Center. I would like to thank the Donner Foundation in Canada and Gustavo Cisneros for additional funding.

A final thanks to Katherine Leiken for her wise advice on organizing the meeting and for her compassion when it all seemed too much.

RSL

Foreword

Vice President Al Gore

The United States Vice President's official residence — where I hosted the Encuentro Group for dinner — was once the house of the superintendent of the United States Naval Observatory. From up on Observatory Hill — above the dust and fogs of the Potomac River bottom — astronomers looked out into the stars, searching for new ways to improve methods of navigation.

One might say that there was something of that same spirit in what these authors and their colleagues were trying to accomplish with the discussion they had on "A New Moment in the Americas." They came together to look back on the many leagues we Americans have already travelled and to chart a course into the future. I assured them that, in thinking about these things, they could assume that the United States will follow a steady course toward closer relations with our neighbors in this hemisphere.

We are determined to sail ahead toward the opportunities we have at the Summit of the Americas this year: the opportunities to strengthen and redefine our ties to the other countries and peoples of the New World.

The changes we are watching in the Americas are among the most revolutionary and promising that we will see in our lifetimes. True, in our hemisphere we haven't seen the walls being torn down or the massive statues being toppled. But the change is no less profound.

It may be that it is somewhat harder to see because, above all else, it has been a cultural change.

Change takes different forms in different places; it's happening both here in North America and in South America. So perhaps the central — and most intriguing — question before the Encuentro Group was, "Are these changes moving us all in a similar direction?" Is what we are seeing a kind of hemispheric convergence?

In Latin America, authoritarian regimes of the right and the left have yielded to open, market economies. What was a somewhat defensive nationalism is being overcome by a new kind of nationalism which stresses possibility over dependency, one that welcomes relations with the United States.

The United States is becoming a more culturally and ethnically diverse society. Latino immigrants are playing a large part in this development.

Through travel, education, and remarkable advances in electronic communications, we see and hear a lot more from one another. You may recall that Uruguayan writer José Enrique Rodó argued that we represent two very different cultural types: a "Calibán" — the hardheaded, pragmatic, but cold Norteamericano — and an "Ariel" — the more spiritual, elegant, but possibly ineffectual Latino.

If there ever was truth to these archetypes, they are certainly not valid today. Though differences still remain, we share so many of the same concerns and issues. Both our regions face the implacable demands of economic globalization and international competition. Both share the social problems of market economies: how to combine justice and enterprise; how to preserve the environment while promoting development. Both share the challenge — and enjoy the benefits — of communications between diverse cultures. Both must cope with differences among our peoples: ethnic, religious, gender, and racial differences. And both face the problems of crime.

These days, democracy is acclaimed everywhere. But sometimes, unfortunately, our democracies seem to rest on ineffective public institutions and on weak civic cultures. History has shown all too often that founding a democracy does not guarantee that it will last.

What are the obstacles to democratic development? How is a democratic civic culture to be built?

One thing that we are beginning to understand more clearly is that the success of both democracy and the market economy depends on the cultural spirit that animates and sustains them. In the case of democracy, the citizens must possess what Alexis de Toqueville called the "habits of the heart": tolerance, a sense of personal responsibility, a willingness to participate. The market economy depends on enterprise, diligence, and a kind of faith in one's commercial partners — the "spirit of democratic capitalism" that Michael Novak has so well described.

The Encuentro Group asked important questions: "Have the old cultural differences — even antagonism — between the North and South Americas begun to give way to a new temper? Is this a temper that can sustain democracy and the free economy? Can we discuss our mutual concerns within a common frame of reference? Can we now find ways to reconcile our remaining differences without the rancor and suspicion that have too often seeped into our relations in the past?"

In short, is there a "New Moment in the Americas?"

The Summit of the Americas takes as its premise that the answer is yes, we are indeed living a "new moment" in the hemisphere, and its purpose is to contribute to the transformation of this "new moment" into a prolonged era of cooperative action among the peoples of the Americas. The essays prepared for this "Encuentro" are themselves an important contribution to this historic transformation.

Introduction

Robert S. Leiken

Vice President Al Gore and former Sandinista Vice President Sergio Ramírez, the parish priest who founded "liberation theology" and a pro-capitalist theologian from the American Enterprise Institute, a choreographer from the West Indies and an Argentine pollster, American historians and sociologists, Mexican journalists and authors, political leaders and political scientists, novelists, economists, critics, playwrights, pundits, poets, and philosophers from left, right, and center and from all around the hemisphere — what made all these different personalities gather to talk of "a new moment in the Americas?"

The spread of democracy in Latin America, the opening of closed economies, and the signing of historical trade agreements are part of the metamorphosis. But the change is not only political, economic, and technological: it is broader and deeper, encompassing demography and disposition, ideas and culture.

The new spirit is remarkable in a region previously divided by geography and cultural heritage, by historical perspective and economic and political systems. Our hemisphere's "new moment" created the conditions for a different kind of conversation, an opportunity to discuss candidly the common problems, hopes, and frustrations of market economies, democratic polities, and global communications and to explore the current state of culture in the hemisphere. We hoped that such a discussion might provide a broad historical and cultural context for the upcoming Summit of the Americas.[1]

The conversation commenced at a dinner, which Vice President Gore hosted at his Washington residence on Friday evening November 11, and then continued at the State Capitol building in Annapolis, Maryland.

At the vice president's residence, according to a *Washington Post* report:

> To the astonishment of the participants, Gore organized the chairs, in encounter group style, in tight circles in the living room. The guests were [asked] whether they believe Latin American and U.S. officials will discover common ground.[2]

To be seated in a circle, each with equal time, was an altogether fitting way to begin the conversation we wished. As if to provide another symbol of the "new moment," Gustavo Gutierrez, the father of Latin American liberation theology and, at times, a stern critic of the United States, gave the blessing over the dinner.

But contrary to some expectations, the mood did not turn contentious. In fact, Rolando Cordera, a Mexican journalist and political figure, told the group, "For the first time in our memory 'interamericanism,' even 'Panamericanism,' are not dirty words...." James Lemoyne, the former *New York Times* bureau chief in Central America, marvelled at the civil, even cordial atmosphere.

Nobody talked about 'imperialism'; nobody talked about anti-Americanism, about 'the revolution,' about coup d'etats and armies. That was not possible five, even three, years ago.

How has our hemisphere arrived at this point?

The New Latin America

The misnamed "Latin American debt crisis" was actually something far more profound and significant. In that period, the entire political and economic structure inherited from Spanish colonialism finally collapsed. What took its place was not merely a series of "economic adjustments" but the rudiments of a new social, political, and cultural order which involved a very different way of looking at the world.

During the so-called "lost decade" of the 1980s, Latin Americans liberated themselves from bureacratic and mercantile states which siphoned wealth extracted from productive sectors to "caudillos" claiming to represent various sectors of society. Not only did this system of clientage, this quasi-corporativist alliance, insulate the economy from foreign competition and thereby retard economic development, but it stymied democratic participation as well.

Thus, what we know as "privatization," "economic adjustment," and "export-led growth" were part of what Beatrice Rangel, the Venezuelan economist, calls Latin America's "most profound political and economic revolution since Independence." That nonviolent democratic revolution produced, according to Manuel Mora y Araujo, Latin America's most prominent public opinion analyst, not only economic reform but the foundation of legitimate democratic regimes, the incorporation of large sectors of the population into political life, and the peaceful resolution of endemic conflicts.

According to Enrique Iglesias, the president of the Inter-American Development Bank (IDB), these "endogenous factors" or internal changes were linked to "exogenous" ones. The process of globalization pushed Latin American countries to pursue economic reforms at home. At the same time, opening their economies to the world buttressed the fragile democracies. As Iglesias explaines, "authoritarian adventures are more risky" when world opinion can influence prosperity so directly. As he points out, this is no small matter in a region known for its abrupt political oscillations. And this buttressing effect was yet another way in which economic reform was joined to political democracy.

As Latin America's economies opened to the world, they opened to one another. Regional economic integration has led to regional political cooperation and to a whole new Latin American culture of integration.

Latin America's chronic inflations may be a thing of the past. Moreover, Mora y Araujo points out that fiscal stability, along with the dismantling of statist economies, was accompanied generally by strong popular support. (The recent election in Brazil, in which the architect of Brazil's anti-inflationary policies won a resounding victory, serves to ratify this trend.) Mora y Araujo also states that these "enormous changes in the political life of our nations" took place "along lines similar to those which have become familiar in much of the world." But Latin Americans' support for painful austerity measures may suggest a broader consensus for both democracy and capitalism than is the case in some parts of Eastern Europe and the former Soviet Union.

Beatrice Rangel sees no turning back from democracy, though, along with many of her colleagues, she worries about the uneven rule of law and access to the legal system in Latin America. Yet she believes economic development is building a "middle-class culture," the bedrock of democracy, while capitalist development will enable Latin America to confront poverty for the first time.

Others at Annapolis were less certain. As the U.S. sociologist Seymour Martin Lipset writes, "[a] transition to democracy does not...assure its institutionalization or permanence." And some of Rangel's colleagues from the South, such as Ramírez, Monsiváis, Father Gutierrez, and Rex Nettleford, were less confident that poverty can be vanquished by an expanding market economy.

All the Latin Americans seemed to agree that formerly marginalized sectors had begun to organize themselves in civic associations. But though Rangel writes that voter participation is increasing in Latin America, Mora y Araujo finds widespread political apathy, especially among the young. However, he also notes that even these alienated Latin Americans do not question the basic values of democracy, which he defines as representative government, equality before the law, and limited power.

There was unanimity about Latin America's new ideological climate. Following what he calls "the irrationalities of populism," Iglesias perceives a turn toward reasonableness. Or, as Carlos Monsiváis, a Mexican intellectual from the Left, puts it: "part of new moment is that we ceased to believe in revolution, in socialism, and in authoritarianism." Maria Elena Cruz Varela, the exiled Cuban poet, was pleased that Cuba was no longer "the center of all discussions" but also sad it is ignored.

That was another way of saying that if yesterday's Latin American discussions focused on civil war, dictatorship, and economic crisis, now the talk was about how to achieve justice, democracy, and economic growth. But the New York writer Paul Berman, echoing Cordera and Ramírez, cautioned us to bear in mind that post-Cold War euphorias have been followed by letdowns.

'Ecumenical America'

At the same time, Latin Americans may not fully appreciate changes that have been taking place in the United States.

The face of the United States has changed dramatically in the past several decades. Latinos have been in the forefront of this metamorphosis and now constitute more than 10 percent of the U.S. population, concentrated in some of the most dynamic regions of the country. Latino immigrants and their descendants play a conspicuous and growing role in the economic, political, and cultural life of the United States. Paul Berman observes that Hispanic culture has been regarded as a "building block" of U.S. culture since the time of Walt Whitman and Henry Wadsworth Longfellow.

By virtue of this increasing interaction of "people, wealth, ideas, and cultural patterns," Harvard sociologist Orlando Patterson observes,"America itself has been radically transformed." Regions of the United States and neighboring countries have formed what Patterson calls "regional cosmoses." There is a "West Atlantic cosmos," which links much of the Eastern United States with the Caribbean and Central America; a "Tex-Mex cosmos," which incorporates Mexican, Native American, and the Southwestern U.S. cultures; a "Southern California cosmos" in which Latin, Asian, African, and European cultures form "a volatile, unblended mosaic"; as well as a "Pacific Rim cosmos" emerging in the Northwest. The product of this mixing and blending is an "ecumenical America," which has produced "the first genuinely global culture on the face of the earth."

While they took some pride in this increasing diversity, North American participants were considerably less sanguine on the state of their democracy.[3] In their essays, the sociologist Seymour Martin Lipset and the political philosopher Jean Bethke Elshtain present impressive evidence that Americans vote less and participate less — not only in politics, but even in such previously typical forms of civic engagement as volunteer and charity organizations, literary and sports groups, fraternal clubs, neighborhood bodies, parent-teacher associations, and labor unions. Lipset shows that Americans distrust their government, the two-party system, and one another at record levels. Elshtain decries a breakdown of the family, generating "unparented children who attend schools that increasingly resemble deten-tion homes rather than centers of enduring training, discipline, and education and contributing to out-of-wedlock births and violence at unprecedented levels." This erosion of sociability has been accompanied, not surprisingly, by corrosive, if technologically advanced, forms of isolation, boredom, despair, and violence. Newspapers are read less and television watched more.

The loss of self-confidence and civic involvement in the hemisphere's preeminent democracy is of special concern for Latin America. As Octavio Paz has pointed out, the United States' democratic spirit "has intervened in our behalf more than once."[4] But that democratic spirit, as the theologian Michael Novak suggested, folds a silver lining into this country's darker moods:

> The North Americans are anxious, needy, worried about the 21st century. Two-thirds think the country is on the wrong track. And that makes us considerably less arrogant than our historical record.

Victorious in the Cold War, but anxious about the future, the United States has now become more open to criticism and counsel. A bipartisan hospitality toward democratic partners and strong support for human rights appear to be superseding the older "hegemonic presumption" of the United States in this hemisphere.

Supporting the North American Free Trade Agreement (NAFTA), Paz notes the emergence of economic (and eventually, he believed, political and cultural) communities in Europe and the Pacific. He affirms, "The general movement of history leads us to regional and continental forms of political and economic association."[5] Latin America faced the choice of "association or historical solitude." Association, Paz argues, was in Latin America's interest: It would promote economic development, advance democracy, and strengthen the weaker nations while constraining the exercise of unilateral power by the United States.

Paz notes that the French and the Germans "had murdered each other for two centuries," and European countries had invaded and occupied one another on multiple occasions, yet

> today all these nations seek not to forget but to transcend these defeats, humiliations, and crimes. The abnormal persistence of certain historical wounds — the Conquest, the war of 1847 [when the United States occupied Mexico] — are not signs of vigor but of uncertainty and insecurity. It is a psychic illness no less pernicious than the loss of historical memory.[6]

Other Novelties of the New Moment

The Mexican-American writer Richard Rodriguez spoke of the new moment being "a moment of great cultural forces meeting." At the last Summit of the Americas, the Conference of American Presidents in Punta del Este in 1967, in the opening line of his keynote speech, the president of Ecuador invoked José Enrique Rodó's *Ariel.* That was a time when the tide of regional conflict was flowing in. Rodó, a Uruguayan philosopher, had written that a "certain robust primitivism" in the United States had devolved into a vulgar, venal, mechanistic, philistine, "universal semi-culture."[7] The bestial North American Calibán dominated Latin America's gentle, spiritual Ariel, a being enlightened by European culture and sense of hierarchy. Rodó's "thesis was repeated excessively and filled the body of theories in our literature for years," the exiled Cuban novelist Heberto Padilla complained at Annapolis.

In the essay that follows in this volume, Paz argued that the "really fundamental difference" between Mexico and the United States is not "the well-known opposition between development and underdevelopment, wealth and poverty, power and weakness, domination and dependence." Each of these "two distinct versions of Western civilization" represents "a unique and precious vision of mankind." In other writings, Paz has urged that the new relationship between us should include "cultural cooperation" but cautions that "culture and tradition change more slowly than ideas and technology."[8]

Paz writes that the Americas displayed a "North-South duality" from the very beginning. The Conquest simply grafted "the new opposition between English and Spaniards...onto the old opposition between nomadic and settled peoples...." In the North would prevail the work ethic, enterprise, the critical spirit, democracy, and capitalism; in the South, hierarchy, ritualism, centralism, orthodoxy, dogmatism, and patrimonialism. In the South, labor was considered servile, identity defined by the ascriptive group or caste into which one was born. The South stressed communal values; the United States, the individual.

Even Paz's archetypes, historically richer, less tendentious than those of Rodó, are challenged from various angles by many of the essays written for the New Moment meeting. Some of the characteristics Paz cites may have migrated. For example, is Latin America becoming more individualistic and the United States more preoccupied with group identities (of gender, race, nationality, or sexual orientation)? Lipset and Elshtain find Americans are less confident, while Latin Americans, according to Rangel,

> are eagerly embracing modernity. Nationalist sentiments, suspicions about the outside world, as well as doubts about our own capacities are disappearing. In their place, we see a growth of self-confidence and a desire to change.

Some of her colleagues at Annapolis, as well as the essays by Ramírez and Monsiváis, suggested that Rangel's statement may be too sweeping. Urbanization, capitalism, and commercial culture have brought to many Latin Americans a thoroughly modern kind of isolation and marginalization, unrelieved by extended families or traditional communities. But even if not all Latin Americans can embrace the future eagerly, many now do. At Annapolis, even the pessimistic Rodriguez, acknowledged that

> my Latin American colleagues have travelled several thousand miles north to speak about the new democratic spirit in their countries, the new spirit of individualism.

The new moment may bring a revision of the stereotypes of the "can-do" American and the brooding or ethereal Latin, immobilized by the past.

There was another challenge to the old "North-South" duality at Annapolis. Several participants spoke of the hemisphere as a culturally mestizo, politically democratic, blend. Nettleford declared that the hemisphere is composed of "cross-fertilized beings. We are all creoles...."

Stanley Crouch writes,

> We have been inside each other's bloodstreams, pockets, libraries, kitchens, schools, theaters, sports arenas, dance halls, and national boundaries for so long that our mixed-up and multiethnic identity extends from European colonial expansion and builds upon immigration.

For Crouch this hemispheric gumbo not only proves but embodies the Enlightenment ideal and stretches it beyond the merely abstract notion of human commonality.

The argot of the new moment was fusion, blending, symbiosis, 'criolization,' symmetry, and reciprocity not North-South division and fixed cultural properties. But, not everyone adopted this language or accepted the larger claims for the new moment.

The New Moment Signifies Common Problems

No one wished to suggest that the new moment brings bliss and harmony. The participants held only that the Americas now confront similar problems and opportunities (albeit with unequal resources) and that, thus, we no longer must discuss our problems from the perspective of a "North-South duality."

Fernando Cepeda, the Colombian diplomat and political scientist, observed that the so-called Latin American drug problem results from organized international crime. The Chilean-American novelist Elena Castedo raised the problem of families, parenting, and children, as women through-out the hemisphere enter the labor force.

Indeed, as Latin America modernizes, it comes to share the problems of societies such as the United States. Rodriguez was moved by "the loss of the village in Latin America" and the growth of "monster cities" inhabited by isolated individuals. These circumstances help to explain, theologian Michael Novak observed, the rise of Protestantism there as Latin Americans find themselves "without the consolation of the village" and wished to be "addressed by a God who speaks to them as individuals."

By the same token, several North Americans worried about growing isolation in the United States, as "checkbook" lobbying organizations replace membership groups and the social bonds formed by active social engage-ment, while isolated channel surfers or inhabitants of "cyberspace" supplant extended families or town meetings (see the essays by Lipset and Elshtain).

Novak asserted that it was precisely "the art of association" which stands between Rodriguez's loss and the anonymous, isolated masses of the cities:

> Tocqueville said that the first law of democracy is the principle of association. He doubted if there were ten men in France able to practice the principle of association as he had seen it in North America.

> He meant the capacity of individuals to join together to build a school or a city hall or a church. Instead of turning to government, as they did in France, people turned to one another....

While in the United States we see a weakening of civic association, Latin American participants testified to its vigorous growth in their region — especially in poorer neighborhoods.

On both sides of the Rio Grande, political parties seem to be in trouble (see Lipset and Mora y Araujo). But many of the Latin Americans appeared to support Mora y Araujo's belief that modern information technology opens channels for "two-way communication" between leaders and citizens, involving the latter in decision-making.

The Latin Americans tended to see as advanced instruments for democratization the very things (television and opinion polls) that the North Americans hold responsible for many of the problems they describe. Elshtain warns of a modern form of "plebiscitary democracy" by means of surveys, lobbies, and the emerging "electronic democracy" associated most closely with Ross Perot. The result is to shrink both voters and legislators to "passive (albeit angry) consumers or instruments." Harvard philospher Harvey Mansfield says we should be wary of nonelective forms of representation that diminish the role of elections and narrow the "constitutional space" that enables the people "to judge the government. If the government reacts too faithfully to popular will, the people get too close to evaluate it."

Two alternative critiques seemed to arise from these exchanges. Perhaps the Latin Americans are repeating a historical tendency to confuse (in Mansfield's terms) "populism and democracy." But then maybe, in the newly developing democracies of Latin America, the main effect of the media is to inform and involve previously marginalized sectors, while in the North the media may sometimes replace, and thereby discourage, civic engagement.

Shades of Identity

"Now that the Latin Americans come here speaking this language of optimism," Rodriguez explained,

> it is appropriate that I, as a "pocho," as a Californian, now tell you about "darkness."...We of the North, by contrast, have become a dark people. We do not vote. We have lost our optimism.

In elaborating his theme, Rodriguez cast a mesmerizing shadow over Saturday's lunch (see Pocho Pioneers). Rodriguez and many Latin Americans felt that the recent passage of Proposition 187 in California, which cut off social services to illegal immigrants, was aimed at Latinos as another blow to their identity. Yet, in Rodriguez's view, it was the "pocho," who crossed the border, often illegally, who could not identify himself as Mexican or as "American," who was the first to discover the new moment. And he was also the first to feel its anguish, the sense of lost certainties and vanished identity. Dagoberto Gilb, the Mexican American novelist, also told us, with flashes of dry humor, of identity confusion along the border and also how economic insecurity compounded the sense of statelessness.

Political identity or group politics presents itself as one sort of solution to the modern identity crisis, but that approach was roundly rejected by the participants. Cordera said that when identity is unmediated by a sense of common citizenship and becomes a political slogan, it leads "to an internal barbarity within each country." Berkeley's Todd Gitlin writes that while identity politics has represented the justifiable pride of a people gaining a place in the sun, too much cultural energy gets spent "policing the boundaries of distinct identity groups."

Monsiváis teased that "national identity" was "indispensable for symposiums." Or, as Octavio Paz put it, "The famous search for identity is an intellectual pastime, sometimes a business, of unemployed sociologists." But Brazilian journalist Antonio Carlos Pereira encountered identity as an American obsession:

> A few months ago, I was being led through San Francisco by a banker's wife, very concerned with social issues. Suddenly, she asked: "What is your ethnic origin?"

I was astonished. That was a question I had never asked myself. None of my friends had asked me, nor had my enemies!

Identity politics, Canadian journalist Andrew Coyne pointed out, combines a "nihilism" that denies universal truth with a "relativism" passionately affirming "group truths." Novak added:

> You cannot have liberty and civilization if there is not a firm idea of truth. I don't mean that anybody has the Truth. But that we all hold ourselves under the evidence. Otherwise, there's only power and interest.

These criticisms of group politics and ideologies were offered by both Latin Americans and North Americans, from both the Left (Cordera, Monsiváis, Gitlin, and Berman) and the Right (Pereira, Mora y Araujo, Novak, and Coyne). Perhaps the ideological conflict of the new moment will no longer divide along left/right lines but between defenders of universality and reason as against advocates of what Gitlin calls "the identity politics of race, sex, gender, ethnicity, and religion."

The participants asked themselves, how should we regard our group identities? Do they define us, and are they the basic components of democratic participation? Or are they among history's iron wardrobe and best melted down into ore suitable for building democracy?

One root of the controversy derives from the fact that the Americas, as "two opposed versions of Western civilization" (Paz), inherited radically different political ideas. The juridical idea of the state, based on individual citizenship, took root in the North and in parts of the Caribbean. But as part of decolonization, Latin America and much of the Caribbean embraced what Orlando Patterson called the "Germanic notion" of an organic, cultural, and ethnic-based nation. Most participants appeared to agree with Patterson that "One of the important new things about the moment is the idea of a non-ethnically defined state based on citizenship and rights. That the states of this hemisphere are embracing. And that's new."

The question of whether the cross-border movement of population, culture, and information of a "New World Culture" would ratify this view of the state or transcend states altogether, was left to the next day as debate yielded to music on Saturday evening. Stanley Crouch had brought together an all-star and all-Americas jazz combo which embodied this diverse hemisphere: Danilo Perez on piano, Idris Muhammad on drums, John Webber on bass, and Gary Bartz on alto sax. Introducing the group, Crouch offered jazz as an instance of how creative cultures melt down history's barricades. And Crouch also extracted from jazz a likeness to the checks and balances of U.S. constitutional government. When government errs, "when you suffer the blues of government, you play the blues of the constitutional process to relieve yourself of the blues of government."

New World Culture

What in the world is "the New World culture?" Well, it appears to have four dimensions: the revolution in communications; the mestizo, "gumbo" character of the hemisphere; the turn to democracy, and increased cultural and educational contact and cooperation. The satellite dish, the fax machine, the modem, interactive video, and direct dialing are among the innovations wiring the Americas, with more obviously to come. In the works, for example, are plans for a hemispheric "direct television" network. The information and communication revolutions have created the material basis for a dynamic diffusion of ideas and art.

The hemisphere's "common cultural and political elements," Lipset recalled, used to be called "Americanidad." In the view of Japanese-American political philosopher Francis Fukuyama, the cultural pluralism of the Americas results not so much from liberal institutions (which have developed only recently in most of Latin America) but "primarily because these were mainly lands of new settlement and immigrant societies." But, Fukuyama continued,

> as societies do get the institutions right, there will be a liberation of cultural forces which will give the Western Hemisphere a big advantage over Europe. The Europeans are building a museum called the European Community, which will preserve their culture intact: a tremendous mistake this hemisphere is not likely to make.

Perhaps the equivalent of cultural free trade could realize Paz's desire for intercourse between the "two versions" of the Americas. But is the "New World Culture" a cross-pollination, a two-way street (as Orlando Patterson argues in his essay below) or is it the realization of Rodó's greatest fear: a leveraged buy-out, an absorption into the "universal semi-culture," the deadening homogenization Monsiváis describes below, one in which (as the U.S. Latin American specialist Mark Falcoff put it) "the culture of the center overtakes and even changes the language of another area."

The salsa, the samba, the meringue, reggae, and jazz are examples of how American influence is part of a reciprocal heightening of popular cultural production within the Americas. Francisco Weffort explained that though the Brazilian samba was born in Rio de Janeiro, it actually became a national music "only because a U.S. record company broadcast it throughout the whole territory." Castedo chimed in that "a Portuguese woman, Carmen Miranda, popularized samba in the United States and all over the world."

Patterson's favorite example is reggae which began as "a pathetic imitation of American rhythm and blues." But soon it fused with local West Indian musical traditions to produce the hybrid. This reggae was then to influence British music and eventually became a major source for American rap.

Other participants had different accounts of and perspectives on creative cultural fusions and confusions. Crouch told how Gabriel García Marquez appropriated William Faulkner for the purposes of his "magic realism."

Lipset noted the wide popularity of Disney productions and of *Reader's Digest* (which "outsold every magazine written in Finnish in Helsinki, every magazine written in Spanish in Buenos Aires, every magazine written in Tagalog in the Philippines"). But, he argued, it did not follow that those who enjoyed American pop culture were thereby Americanized. It merely signified that Americans were first and most efficient in reaching a common, worldwide popular taste.

"American culture did not have to impose itself upon the world," Cepeda agreed.

> It has seduced the world. People want to be like the United States, even if they don't like the United States. It's very strange. Everybody wants to be like Americans. It is a popular culture. It is not aristocratic.

But Monsiváis and Gitlin replied that American cultural success was the result of corporate investment, "an industrial process (not a seduction)" which exercised what Monsiváis called "a dictatorship of taste." Patterson responded that views such as those reflected "the propagandistic reaction of traditional cultural gatekeepers in Third World societies."

There was no consensus on the old question as to whether cultural diffusion means a decline to "a universal semi-culture" or invigorates and even raises the mean level of all cultures. But there was a consensus that a creative hemispheric cultural community could not be planned: Culture is, inevitably, spontaneous. However, there was also general agreement that if cultural enrichment was the product of "many interrelations," as Cordera concluded, one of those "will be international communication." Specifically, Cordera proposed that "one component we could plan, or at least induce, would be the transmission of basic values: democracy, human rights, legitimate representation, and accountability." "Let's get on the Internet," Coyne concluded jovially.

A New Conversation

In my view, the conversation in Annapolis represented a departure in several ways. No one could remember such a broad group of cultural and intellectual leaders from around the hemisphere meeting so civilly to discuss such controversial issues. Moreover, gone was the tired rhetoric, the breast-beating and recriminations that have characterized inter-American discourse for a generation. Instead, there were congeniality, civility, and candor. At times, the candor was striking, as when Father Gutierrez declared:

> Latin Americans don't like to say that there is racism in Latin America. We are very embarrassed by it. What we don't have are racist laws. Why would you when laws are not respected? What we have in Latin America is racist mores, racist customs.

The Americans were equally forthcoming, as we have seen, in exposing the problems of their own somewhat demoralized civic and political life.

Vice President Gore summed the meeting up in a useful way. In an address to the Organization of American States, he recalled "the rich, important — and absorbing — discussion" he had hosted. He pointed out that the diverse group in that discussion "agreed on one major idea: that there is right now what some have called a 'New Moment in the Americas' — a point in history that offers more hope than any other in our long history." Gitlin, the former student radical, contrasted this meeting to other contemporary scenes in which "people are burning bridges" rather than building them:

> Our moment has to be created through conversations. I know conversations are "talky," but we don't have any better way. Either this or war. This is a lot better.

The hope was expressed that our own conversation can be a metaphor for emerging hemispheric relations: a place where all are heard and are free to agree or disagree, where no single point of view governs, in which differences are settled by persuasion not coercion, or, if not settled, left to be discussed on another occasion.

Notes

1.   This volume is based on essays prepared for that conversation by several of the thirty cultural and intellectual leaders who participated. This account attempts both to summarize the three-day "encuentro" — to the extent that such a rich and wide-ranging encounter could be summarized in a rapid report — and to introduce the essays that follow.

We also include an essay by Octavio Paz, who, although he could not be with us for reasons of health, nevertheless remained a towering intellectual presence at the meeting. Harvey C. Mansfield of Harvard University also was unable to attend but was kind enough to submit an essay to this volume which also informed our discussions. Richard Rodriguez's "Pocho Pioneer" was originally an address delivered to the meeting and then edited by him. The remarks of Enrique Iglesias were also part of an address which unfortunately could not be included here due to time constraints.

2.   Al Kamen, "Despite Defeat, an Upbeat Dinner Debate," *Washington Post*, November 21, 1994, A23.

3.   Rex Nettleford observed that the United States had "hi-jacked" the word American, which properly belongs to the entire hemisphere. Others have argued that its use is appropriate because only the United States of America uses the term in its proper name. In this essay, I shall use the term American in referring to citizens of the United States. If we employ the term to describe citizens of the United States, I do so with apologies and only to avoid clumsy neologisms.

4.   Octavio Paz, "Panamá y otros palenques." In *Pequeña Crónica de Grandes Días*, Fondo de Cultura Económica, Mexico 1990:52.

5.   Octavio Paz, "América: ¿Comunidad o coto redondo?" In *Pequeña Crónica...*, 44.

6.   Paz 1990, 51-53.

7.   José Enrique Rodó, *Ariel*, University of Texas Press, Austin, Texas, 1988: 76, 79-83, 85, 98.

8.   Paz, "Panama...", *op. cit.:* 55.

Elena Castedo, Francis Fukuyama, Todd Gitlin, and Heberto Padilla

Rolando Cordera Campos, Enrique Iglesias, and Sergio Ramírez

"A New Moment in the Americas" took place in the Calvert Room at the State House in Annapolis, Maryland.

Maria Elena Cruz Varela, Richard Rodriguez, Michael Novak, and Dagoberto Gilb.

Rex Nettleford and Beatrice Rangel Mantilla

Seymour Martin Lipset

Carlos Monsiváis and Sergio Ramírez

Introduction

Dagoberto Gilb and Stanley Crouch

Orlando Patterson

Contributors and Participants

Elena Castedo, Chile-United States. Essayist, poet, novelist, and editor of the *The Inter-American Review of Bibliography*, her debut novel, *Paradise*, was nominated for the 1990 National Book Award and for the Cervantes prize in Spain. She has published essays, articles, poetry, and fiction in Spanish and English. Her first short story received Phoebe's 1986 prize for best fiction of the year, and her second was a winner of the 1991 PEN/Syndicated fiction award. Born in Spain, she was raised in Chile and is now living in Massachusetts.

Stanley Crouch, United States. Actor, playwright, poet, director, and essayist, he is founder of Jazz at Lincoln Center whose music criticism and essays have appeared in *Harper's*, *The New York Times*, *Vogue*, *Downbeat*, and *The New Republic*. His *Notes of a Hanging Judge* was nominated for an award by the National Book Critics Circle and selected by the *Encyclopedia Britannica Yearbook* as the best book of essays for 1990. A recipient of both the Jean Stein Award from the American Academy of Arts and Letters and a MacArthur Foundation grant, he is writing scripts for an eight-part television miniseries on jazz and is awaiting publication of a biography of Charlie Parker, a new collection of jazz essays and reviews, and an epic novel.

Jean Bethke Elshtain, United States. A political philosopher who focuses on the connections between politics and ethics, she is currently Centennial Professor of Political Science at Vanderbilt University and will become Laura Spelman Rockefeller Professor of Social and Political Ethics at the University of Chicago in January. She has published extensively on contemporary social, political, military, family, and women's issues, including some three hundred reviews and several books, including *Public Man, Private Woman: Women in Social and Political Thought* and *Women and War*. Her latest book, *Democracy on Trial*, is to be published by Basic Books in January.

Todd Gitlin, United States. Professor of sociology and director of the mass communications program at the University of California at Berkeley, he is the author of six books, including *The Sixties: Years of Hope, Days of Rage; Inside Prime Time; The Whole World is Watching;* a novel, and a collection of poetry. He has received numerous writing awards and grants, including those from the MacArthur Foundation, the National Endowment for the Humanities, and the Rockefeller Foundation. He is published widely in both general and scholarly journals and is currently working on a second novel.

Seymour Martin Lipset, United States. A widely cited sociologist, he has also been judged the most cited living political scientist, according to an article in *Political Science*. He is currently Hazel Professor of Public Policy at the George Mason University Institute of Public Policy and Senior Scholar of the Progressive Policy Institute and the Woodrow Wilson Center. The prize-winning author of *Political Man, The Politics of Unreason*, and *The First New Nation*, among other books, he has been elected to the National Academy of Sciences and has served as President of both the American Sociological Association and the American Political Science Association.

Harvey C. Mansfield, United States. William R. Kenan, Jr. Professor of Government at Harvard University, Mr. Mansfield is President of the New England Political Science Association and has been a member of the Advisory Council of the National Endowment for the Humanities. His books include *America's Constitutional Soul, Taming the Prince: The Ambivalence of Modern Executive Power, Machiavelli's Florentine Histories*, and a new translation of *Machiavelli's The Prince*.

Carlos Monsiváis Aceves, Mexico. Social commentator, novelist, playwright, writer, and philosopher, this well-known Mexican intellectual has published numerous books and edited several anthologies of contemporary Mexican poetry. Among his books are *Días de guardar, Nuevo catecismo para indios remisos*, and *Entrada libre: Crónicas de la sociedad que se organiza*.

Manuel Mora y Araujo, Argentina. Latin America's most prominent public opinion pollster, he is a specialist in politics, public opinion, market research, and communications. He is a columnist for *La Nacion* and other Argentine and foreign periodicals, and among his various books are *The Peronist Vote*, an interpretation of the origins and structure of Peronism, and *Liberalism and Democracy*, a collection of essays on contemporary politics.

Orlando Patterson, United States. A native of Jamaica, he is presently serving as John Cowles Professor of Sociology at Harvard University. He is author of seven books and book-length reports on topics of urban poverty, race, and ethnicity (including "ethnic chauvinism") and the history and legacy of slavery. He has also published three novels, and his first volume of a two-volume work entitled *Freedom in the Making of Western Culture* won the National Book Award in 1991. His current area of interest is how problems of race, immigration, and multiculturalism intersect in the contemporary United States.

Octavio Paz, Mexico. Preeminent intellectual, poet, and cultural commentator, he was awarded the Nobel Prize in Literature in 1990 for his corpus of work which spans over six decades. Mr. Paz is known throughout the world, and his work has appeared in Spanish and numerous other languages. He has served in the diplomatic service of Mexico as Ambassador to India and other diplomatic posts.

Sergio Ramírez Mercado, Nicaragua. Former Vice President of Nicaragua, lawyer, current leader of the *Sandinista* bloc in the National Assembly of Nicaragua, and a major Latin American novelist and essayist, he is a former student activist, writer, party intellectual, and revolutionary leader of the FSLN (Sandinista National Liberation Front). During the Somoza dictatorship, he lived and wrote while in exile in Costa Rica and West Berlin. He is co-founder of the literary movement *Ventana*.

Beatrice Rangel Mantilla, Venezuela. Former chief of staff to the president, public administrator, and economist, she has provided nearly 25 years of service to the government of Venezuela. She has held senior positions in the Ministry of Foreign Relations, the Ministry of the Presidential Secretariat, the Ministry of Education, and the National Congress.

Richard Rodriguez, United States. His celebrated autobiography, titled *Hunger of Memory*, was published in 1982, and his second book, *Days of Obligation: An Argument with My Mexican Father*, was one of three finalists for a Pulitzer Prize in nonfiction in 1993. Other awards include an Emmy for Short Historical Essay, the NEH Frankel Medal, the International Journalism Award from the World Affairs Council of California, and the NEH and Fulbright fellowships. He is currently an editor with the Pacific News Service in San Francisico, essayist for the *MacNeil/Lehrer News Hour*, and contributing editor for *Harper's, The Los Angeles Times,* and *U.S. News and World Report*.

Coordinator and editor: **Robert S. Leiken**, United States. The coordinator of "A New Moment in the Americas" and editor of the resulting volume of essays, Mr. Leiken has been a Research Associate at the Harvard University Center for International Affairs, a Senior Associate at the Carnegie Endowment for International Peace, and a Senior Fellow at the Georgetown University Center for Strategic and International Studies. He has been Professor of History at Centro de Investigación y Docencia Económica in Mexico. Mr. Leiken is co-editor of *The Central American Crisis Reader* and the editor of *Central America: Anatomy of a Conflict* and has published in journals such as *The New York Review of Books, The Times Literary Supplement,* and *The New Republic*.

Moderators: **Mark Falcoff**, United States; **James LeMoyne**, United States; **Julia Preston**, United States.

Participants: **Paul Berman**, United States; **Fernando Cepeda Ulloa**, Colombia; **Rolando Cordera Campos**, Mexico; **Andrew Coyne**, Canada; **Maria Elena Cruz Varela**, Cuba-United States; **James Fallows**, United States; **Francis Fukuyama**, United States; **Dagoberto Gilb**, United States; **Gustavo Gutiérrez**, Peru; **Rex Nettleford**, Jamaica; **Michael Novak**, United States; **Heberto Padilla**, Cuba-United States; **Antonio Carlos Pereira**, Brazil; **Francisco Weffort**, Brazil; The authors, with the exception of Octavio Paz and Harvey C. Mansfield, also participated at "A New Moment in the Americas."

Section I

————————

State and Civil Society

————————

Chapter 1

American Democracy in Comparative Perspective

Seymour Martin Lipset

Following the spread of democracy in the past two decades, the problems of political transition have become a major subject for thought and writings the world over. Dictatorships and authoritarian regimes are being replaced throughout Southern Europe, Latin America, much of the former communist world, and to some extent Africa. The stable polities of the affluent Free World — those of Northern Europe, North America, and Australasia — are held up as models for the emerging democracies. The older send missions to help organize political parties, run elections, and, of course, reform economies. Yet the governability of the established democracies is in question as the demands on them grow. Opinion polls from all the nations of Europe, except Luxembourg, plus those in North America and Australasia, find that large majorities lack confidence in their political leaders and institutions. In particular, the difficulties experienced by the oldest electoral democracy, the United States, force us, as Michel Crozier has noted, to reappraise "the working and limits of democratic government," to react to developments, which, as E.J. Dionne, Jr., has brilliantly documented, demonstrate that democracy "is decaying in the United States."

A transition to democracy does not, of course, assure its institutional-ization or permanence. Efforts to create democracy have frequently failed, as the history of most nations in this hemisphere and throughout the world reveals. In 1920, 20 of the 26 European states were parliamentary democracies; by 1938, only 12 were. The tensions of transition, the weakness of regime legitimacy, and recurrent economic breakdowns and/or widespread poverty led to the collapse of most new democracies established after World Wars I and II in Europe and Latin America and in various new nations in Africa and Asia —hence, the production of a considerable literature dealing with the experiences of failed or unstable democratic polities.

The Fragile Party System

One of the most disturbing trends is a widespread decline in the strength of political parties. As Joseph Schumpeter noted, the principal way in which the masses can affect the composition and policies of governments is through their ability to choose freely between organized alternatives, i.e., parties. Alarmingly, institutionalized political parties in the older free polities are becoming increasingly fragile. Electorates around the world have become much more volatile, less loyal to established parties, and more prone to shift among them. And yet, as Schumpeter and Stein Rokkan emphasized, strong partisan loyalties, which can survive political disasters, are a necessary condition for stable democracy.

A decline in such commitments could spell the demise of parties, as has happened often in emerging democracies, whose new organizations necessarily lack a loyal base. The Federalist party, one of the first two parties in the United States, lost power in 1800 and soon ceased to be a major contender for presidential office. This phenomenon has also occurred on a number of occasions in post-authoritarian regimes as diverse as post-Franco Spain, East Germany, and Poland, where Solidarity, which once had ten million members, is now a shadow of its past self. Such developments reflect the fact that new parties generally cannot count on a strong base of loyalty.

Even older, more established democratic systems are not immune. The previously dominant Conservative Party of Canada declined to 16 percent of the vote and two seats in parliament in 1993. In Italy, scandals have nearly eliminated the two leading parties, the Christian Democrats and the Socialists. The French Socialists, who were able to elect François Mitterrand as president twice during the 1980s, appear now to have lost most of their strength.

Widespread Cynicism in the Electorate

The weakening of the party is but one indicator that even well-established democracies are facing difficulties. Across the democratic world, opinion polls show that the citizenry are increasingly distrustful of their political leaders and institutions. When asked about their "confidence" in government, large majorities in almost every country report they have "none," "little," or "a fair amount" of trust in the prime minister or president and the legislative bodies. The strongly positive are minorities, usually small ones.

The United States provides a striking example of this breakdown of respect for authority. Confidence in all United States institutions inquired about in the opinion surveys declined precipitously and steadily from the mid-1960s, though the greatest part of the fall occurred early in that decade. The Louis Harris Poll, which has investigated the subject since 1966, reported in 1994 the lowest level of confidence in government institutions ever. Those expressing a "great deal" of confidence in the executive branch of government constituted only 12 percent of a national sample in 1994 as compared to 24 percent in 1981 and 41 percent in 1966. Trust in Congress was even lower — 8 percent in 1994 contrasted with 16 percent in 1981 and 42 percent in 1966. Yankelovich reports a drastic shift for the worse in response to the question "How much of the time can you trust the government to do what's right?" In 1964, 76 percent said "always" or "most of the time." The proportion so answering fell to 44 percent in 1984 and then to an all-time low of 19 percent in 1994, a finding reported in the latest Luntz Poll for the Hudson Institute.

The University of Michigan Survey Research Center's national election study has been asking: "Would you say the government is pretty much run by a few big interests looking out for themselves or that it is run for the benefit of all the people?" In 1964, 29 percent said it was run for a few big interests. By 1980 the proportion so replying had moved up to 70 percent; in 1992, fully four-fifths, 80 percent, expressed this cynical view. A Gallup Poll conducted for the *Times-Mirror* organization in 1994 found that 66 percent of a national sample agreed that the "Government is almost always wasteful and inefficient." A similar percentage said that "most elected officials don't care what people like me think." Again, the data show steady increases in disdain for officeholders. In response to this question, just under half, 47 percent, agreed in 1987, compared to 33 percent in the 1960s.

These doubts manifest themselves in numerous ways, including a decline in voter participation and erosion of the two-party system. The United States, which could once boast that the overwhelming majority of eligible voters cast their ballots, lost that record after 1914 and is experiencing a new pattern of decline. In fact, a much smaller proportion take part in U.S. national elections than in any of the other older democracies, except Switzerland. The percentage voting has fallen from a postwar high point of around two-thirds at the beginning of the 1960s to little more than one-half in presidential elections today. Considerably fewer take part in lower-level contests, state and city elections and even the presidential primaries. In reporting on the most recent of such contests, the mid-term primaries in 1994, the Committee for the Study of the American Electorate noted that only 18 percent of the voting age population cast ballots, compared to 24 percent in 1974 and 33 percent in 1966.

The lack of faith in the traditional U.S. political system also is strikingly revealed by declining regard for the two-party system. In 1994, for the first time in polling history, a majority of those interviewed, 53 percent, told Gallup that they would like to see a third major party. Evidence that this sentiment is not simply symbolic is provided by the support which Ross Perot obtained in the 1992 election and continues to receive in opinion polls in 1994. Perot secured the highest percentage of the vote ever attained by a third-party candidate, with the limited exception of Theodore Roosevelt in 1912. Roosevelt, however, was a dissident Republican preferred in the 12 primaries of that year by most of his party's supporters. The 1994 opinion polls show that Perot continues to be endorsed by a fifth of the electorate.

Legacy of the 1960s

This erosion of trust in U.S. government is troubling. Then President Jimmy Carter characterized it in a July 1979 television address to the American people as a "fundamental threat to American democracy." That threat, he said, was a "crisis of confidence...that strikes at the very heart and soul and spirit of our national will." He pointed to "a growing disrespect for government and for churches and for schools, the news media and other institutions" and emphasized that "the gap between our citizens and our government has never been so wide." If anything, that gap has widened. In a report on a 1994 poll evaluating "The New Political Landscape," the *Times-Mirror* Center finds that

> Voters' frustration with the political system continues to grow, as does animosity toward the media....The Clinton administration and

the economic recovery have failed to stem the tide of political cynicism. The discontent with Washington that gained momentum in the late 1980s is even greater now than it was in 1992.

Other opinion polls indicate that this severe decline in confidence began even earlier, during the mid-1960s, a period characterized by widespread protest, and has continued to the present. (That record has been documented in detail in a book by William Schneider and myself, *The Confidence Gap: Business, Labor, and Government in the Public Mind.*) The catalysts for this dramatic loss of faith in institutions are a combination of reactions to the Vietnam War and the discontent represented by various social movements, initially linked to the antiwar struggles, which severely criticized America for not living up to its democratic and egalitarian promise. These were primarily concerned with race relations, the status of women, and the environment. Previously, alienation or organized protest in Western democratic society had been based largely on the traditionally underprivileged strata, but the movements of the 1960s stemmed mostly from the more affluent classes, university students, professionals, and middle-class women. The one important protest wave that reflected the problems of the underprivileged was, of course, the civil rights campaigns led by Martin Luther King.

Mass protest declined, seemingly almost vanished, with the end of the Vietnam War and the passage of important civil rights legislation, but public opinion research and electoral behavior indicated that a large percentage of Americans continued to feel frustrated with their political leaders and institutions. Events in the next decade, including the economic downswing of the early 1970s and the Watergate scandal, intensified the disdain for political leadership. The Carter years, marked by economic stagnation, high rates of inflation and unemployment, and finally the Iran hostage crisis, did not help.

A partial hiatus in the downward trend in public confidence occurred in the 1980s. Ironically, given his antagonism to government, Ronald Reagan's administration produced an increase in confidence in government in reaction to economic growth and prosperity during most of his term in office. This improvement, however, was relatively minor and did not affect attitudes toward other major institutions, e.g., business and labor. Frustration continued to dominate. In any case, the Reagan blip ended with the Iran-Contra scandal in November 1986. The basically downward trend has continued under Presidents Bush and Clinton, although there was an upswing that proved to be very short-lived after the Gulf War in early 1991. By the summer, it was gone.

Television's Distorting Picture

Why is there so much malaise, so much unrest about the workings of U.S. democracy? The discontent generated in the 1960s does not explain why these feelings have continued or what has sustained them. Politicians tend to blame the media for the lack of trust. I suspect that to some considerable degree they are right. American presidents since George Washington have complained about the way the press covered them. Thomas Jefferson, Andrew Jackson, Abraham Lincoln, and Franklin Roosevelt all correctly felt that much of the press was antagonistic. Those on the left from Jefferson to Roosevelt and Truman felt that the owners of newspapers were conservatives and controlled the way their papers wrote about them. Since Lyndon Johnson, presidents have identified media bias as reflecting the views of journalists, not owners, and as leftist or liberal. There can be little doubt that the predominantly left views of reporters affect the way the news is presented. But the political views or interests of those who dominate the media are not the main sources of their emphasis on the failings of elites and institutions. The fact is that good news is not news; bad news is. Planes that land do not constitute a story; planes that crash do. Politicians characterized by honesty, personal integrity, and a good family life are dull. Sexually promiscuous, corrupt political figures are interesting. The press looks for failings. The desire to locate and exaggerate scandals among the political, social, and economic elites has always characterized open democratic societies.

There has, however, been a change in the nature of the media, which I think is responsible for perpetuating and extending the loss in trust — the shift from print to television as the major source of news. Television presents the news and conveys the message in much stronger terms, in much more convincing fashion than newspapers or magazines. The massive transition from print to televised media occurred in the 1960s. The Vietnam War was the first televised war; for the first time, the public could watch the spilling of blood in their living rooms. The impact of the prolonged war on American opinion was, to a considerable extent, a function of pictorial reportage. And the domination of the camera has continued to grow. All problems of society now reach people almost immediately and in what appears an unbiased manner, because the viewer thinks he sees what is happening for himself. There have been other notable changes as well.

Norman Ornstein has noted that the increase in reportage on scandals and corruption in government and other institutions is linked to greater disclosure. Sweeping reform of the political process has resulted in a drastic increase in information made possible by the computer, which has been grist for investigative journalism. As important in undermining trust in leaders has been the enormous growth in "prosecutorial zeal," flowing in part from "the reform-era creation of a Public Integrity Section in the Justice Department, which defines its success by the volume of prosecution of public officials." As a result, Ornstein reports, between "1975 and 1989, the number of federal officials indicted on charges of public corruption increased by a staggering 1,211 percent, whereas the number of non-federal public officials indicted doubled during the same period." There has clearly been more bad news to report about politics, as well as a more effective medium to transmit it.

Governmental Gridlock

These developments have played an important role in intensifying the problem of "gridlock" that affects American politics. "Gridlock," the inability of our political institutions to respond quickly, is not new, but flows in part from the basic structure of the U.S. government. The Founding Fathers were classical liberals or libertarians who feared and disliked the power of the state. They deliberately made it difficult for political leaders to be effective, as they sought to reduce the powers of the executive. As all Americans know, the authors of the Constitution established a polity characterized by checks and balances, one designed to answer Madison's question of how government can control itself. The president is chosen by the people, not from or by a parliament. There are two almost co-equal legislative bodies, the Senate and the House of Representatives, elected separately and for varying terms. The members of a fourth body, the Supreme Court, are appointed for life terms to interpret legislation and mediate relations among the elected branches of government. The Founding Fathers wanted to make it difficult to enact major reforms, and they succeeded. If they were to return to Washington today, they would recognize our government as the one they planned, although like the rest of us they might be unhappy with some of the effects. One of the most important consequences of the separation of powers is a weak party and governmental system, one in which the executive branch — the administration and the president — has little control over the legislature.

The system differs greatly from that of parliamentary countries such as Britain or Canada, which have disciplined legislative parties. A prime minister with an effective parliamentary majority is much more powerful than an American president; he can secure the enactment of the legislation he and his cabinet support in a short period of time. In the United States, presidents may propose but, as they all learn, Congress disposes. With the weak party discipline of the United States, gridlock occurs even when the president and both congressional bodies nominally belong to the same party. Franklin Roosevelt was overwhelmingly reelected in 1936 with an enlarged congressional majority for the Democrats, yet that Democratic Congress rejected much of the legislation Roosevelt proposed in his second term. Jimmy Carter and now Bill Clinton have each learned that to get Democratic majorities to pass the legislation he wants, he must campaign. Undisciplined congressional parties are not a recent phenomena, although in pre-World War II days presidents and party leaders exerted more influence over members of Congress.

The decline of patronage, the growth of a merit-based civil service and the increasing reliance on primary elections to nominate candidates have further weakened party organizations. In the past, party nominees were designated by conventions of the party faithful interested in securing patronage, rewards, jobs and contracts from the elected officeholders. Today, those who run for president, Congress, or lower office rarely turn to the party organizations. Rather, the road to a nomination via the primaries requires the formation of committees of friends and potential supporters and, most importantly, the raising of money from people interested in political objectives, whether for ideological or special-interest reasons.

The Changing Campaign

The diminished influence of party organizations and leaders, what Americans once called "machines" and "bosses," has expanded the importance of money in U.S. elections. With the emergence of television as the prime campaign medium, candidates, including incumbents, need to raise large sums of money. Close to 60 percent of congressional campaign budgets now pay for broadcast events, compared to 17 percent in the 1950s. Candidates must hire campaign managers, consultants, pollsters, speech writers, and buy television time in two contests, the primary and the general election. The growth in the significance of television has made money more important in politics and has also changed the nature of campaigns. Television presses candidates to speak simply, in few words, leading to a decline in the reporting and discussing of issues. The length of sound bites, reported statements by candidates, has fallen dramatically in tandem with the increasing importance of television. Thomas Patterson reports that by 1988 a candidate's typical sound bite presented in the newscasts was less than 10 seconds. The same was true in 1992. The print media has followed television's lead in reducing the space given to candidate views. Hence, the ever-greater need for nominees to spend money to project their message.

Ironically, the increased need for funds by candidates was accompanied in the 1960s by major campaign reforms. These restrictions on contributions have made the collection of money much more difficult. Because wealthy supporters cannot make big individual contributions, special interests with funds collected from many different individuals are in a stronger position to influence politicians than in the past. Since interest groups providing funds through political action committees are able to influence the actions of members of Congress, particularly to get them to defeat measures, the inherent tendency toward gridlock is intensified.

The failure of the 1994 Clinton proposals for health care reform illustrates the increased impact of money on American policymaking. A complex plan proposed by the president's task force on health care reform was effectively obstructed by myriad organizations and interests, including medical insurance groups and business organizations. Other interest groups such as labor unions heavily lobbied Congress for Clinton's health plan. Hospitals and universities campaigned, both for and against, as well. The result was gridlock.

As the health care episode illustrates, members of Congress must be receptive not only to their constituencies but to fund-raisers and lobbyists as well. The weakening of parties, the ever-growing need to raise campaign funds, and the greater importance of government in the economy have all contributed to the enhancement of the role of the lobbyist. The number of lobbyists doubled from roughly 3,500 to 7,000 in the past 20 years. Lobbyists, of course, are not simply those representing corporations or other monied private interests; public interest lobbies such as environmental and civil rights groups and feminist organizations all exert pressure.

Organized political influence operates somewhat differently in the United States than in other democratic countries. Lobbying individual representatives or legislators in parliamentary countries is much less important than here, since members of parliament in Toronto or Liverpool or Hamburg must support cabinet policy. Those seeking to pass or defeat legislation in such systems must apply pressure on the cabinet or national party leaders.

Waning Civic Engagement

The associations of civil society, which have created networks of communications among people with common positions and interests helping to sustain political parties and political participation, have also declined greatly in the postwar years. This trend, too, has contributed to weakening campaign processes in the established democracies. Early U.S. election research conducted by Paul Lazarsfeld and Angus Campbell in the 1940s and 1950s documented the importance of major structural cleavages such as class, region, religion, and ethnicity in determining where voters stood. But increased education and higher rates of social and geographical mobility have reduced the importance of these factors. Correlations between class position and party voting have dropped in the United States and other countries as well. The great decline in the proportion of the U.S. workforce belonging to trade unions, from 33 percent in 1955 to 16 percent today, has contributed to the reduction of the importance of class in politics. At the same time, various issues less related to class, such as the environment or abortion, have increased in importance. The rise of feminism has also played a role, shifting educated women to the left and economically privileged religious and moral conservatives to the right. With increased assimilation and higher rates of intermarriage, ethnicity and religion have become less important as determinants of political allegiance, although African Americans, Jews, evangelical white Protestants, and the most recent immigrant groupings, particularly Latinos, maintain communal ties to politics.

Beyond the impact of changes in macrostructure is the effect of the shift in the component parts of civil society which Alexis de Tocqueville so emphasized in his classic, *Democracy in America*. Tocqueville was struck by the many voluntary institutions interposed between the citizenry and the state in America and observed that these structures fostered individualism, provided channels of communication, and inhibited the power of government. He was particularly impressed that religion, much stronger here than elsewhere, was not supported by the state and fostered myriad other voluntary groups. Though not political, these groups stimulated community participation, built activist skills, and trained leaders. Tocqueville also emphasized the importance of the institutions of civil society in the creation and maintenance of democratic cultural values and norms.

Robert Putnam, in an important article, "Bowling Alone: Democracy at the End of the Twentieth Century," and Theodore Caplow et al., in *Recent Social Trends in the United States, 1960-1990*, have brought together a large amount of empirical data from different American sources which validate much of Tocqueville's analysis of the impact of group membership on political behavior. Their data also indicate that participation in civil society or "civic engagement," to use Putnam's term, has declined in the past three decades. Putnam contends that America's social capital, "the norms and networks of civic engagement," are weak, that democracy itself is thereby endangered. He sums up his findings by saying that "civic engagement of all sorts has unexpectedly plummeted in the United States over the last generation. Participation in many types of civic associations from religious groups to labor unions, from women's clubs to fraternal clubs and from neighborhood gatherings to bowling leagues has fallen off." And these changes are very important because "research in a wide range of contexts has confirmed that the norms and networks of civic engagement can improve education, diminish poverty, inhibit crime, boost economic performance, foster better government, and even reduce mortality rates" (cited with permission of the author).

Most, but not all, of the available data bear out Putnam's assumptions. A Roper survey taken in August 1993 indicates that the percentage of people who have "attended a public meeting on town or school affairs" has dropped by more than one-third from 23 percent in 1973 to 16 percent in 1993. The proportion who attended a political rally or speech, who served on a committee, or who were officers of a club or organization also fell off over this twenty-year period. All told, those reporting involvement in at least one of six civic activities declined from 50 to 43 percent. Detailed reports in *Recent Social Trends* and Putnam's article provide survey evidence that there has been a drop in membership in church-related groups although not in church attendance. (The issue of participation in religion is an unresolved one since there are conflicting findings in this area.) Americans, however, still bear out Tocqueville's observation that they are among the most devout people in Christendom.

One of the most critical forms of community participation in the United States has been in parent-teacher associations (PTA), reflecting Americans' high commitment to education. Putnam reports a very significant dropoff in membership in the PTA from the 1960s to the present, from 12 million in 1964 to 5 million in 1982, though there is some indication that membership may have rebounded somewhat to 7 million in recent years. *Recent Social Trends* and Putnam also indicate that fraternal and ethnic organizations have experienced a steady decline. The two sources disagree, however, about changes in rates of volunteering. *Recent Social Trends* concludes that they have increased, while Putnam notes a decrease. Gallup polls also find that the proportion indicating that they have volunteered for charitable, "social service," or "nonprofit" organizations has climbed from 27 percent in 1977 to 54 percent in 1989 and but then gone down to 48 in 1994.

Putnam also reports a type of civic organization that has grown in membership in recent years. These are groups like the National Organization of Women, the Sierra Club, and the American Association of Retired People (AARP), which increased from 400,000 dues-paying members in 1960 to 33 million in 1993. But these Putnam sees as essentially lobbying groups, not as Tocqueville's type of civic association. In his view they do not promote "civic engagement" because they are basically what he calls checkbook organizations. Their members pay dues but rarely attend any meetings and seldom, if ever, knowingly encounter other members. They are not mechanisms for communication or the learning of politically relevant skills.

Perhaps as interesting as these findings about participation in organized activities are the reports from National Opinion Research Center (NORC) which indicate that not only has there been an erosion in trust in institutions, but there has been a decline in trust in people. In response to the question, "Some say that most people can be trusted, while others say that you can't be too careful in dealing with people. Which do you believe?", the proportion reporting that most people can be trusted has dropped by more than one-third between 1960 and 1993, from 58 percent to 37 percent.

Putnam discusses various possible causes of these changes, including the movement of women into the labor force, the decline in the size and stability of the family, and high rates of geographic mobility, and finds good reasons to reject these hypotheses. He notes the importance of television in helping to individualize the use of leisure time and points to various time budget studies documenting the steady increase in time devoted to television, which has "dwarfed all of the changes in the way Americans spend their days and nights." Other technological developments have had similar effects. For example, the growth in the technology for listening to music — the cassette tape, compact disc, and the Walkman — have helped privatize Americans and reduced their interpersonal contacts outside work.

The timing of these changes corresponds to the declines which have been reported for civic participation and trust in institutions. NORC finds that the percentage of the population who watch television for only an hour a day or less decreased from 37 in 1964, to 27 in 1978, to 22 in 1989, and then up to 25 in 1993. Those looking at the tube for four hours or more a day climbed from 19 percent in 1964 to 28 in 1993. Conversely, the proportion reading newspapers every day fell from 73 percent in 1967 to 46 in 1993.

In tandem with, or possibly caused by, the decline in confidence in institutions and trust in others, something appears to have been happening since the mid-1960s that has been undermining the civic culture of America. But although these findings suggest that the underlying structures and networks supporting an active political life have declined in America, Putnam also reaffirms Tocqueville's conclusion that Americans are "more trusting and civicly engaged than most other people in the world." But the trend, for the most part, is downward.

Political theorist Robert Dahl, writing in the Fall 1993 issue of the socialist magazine *Dissent*, contends that the decrease in political efficacy and trust in America reflects a "fragmentation" of the political process. By this he means the decline of party organization, inside and outside the government, accompanied by the increase in the sheer number of interest groups and lobbies, and the resultant growing lack of accountability of political leaders.

Paradoxically, the increase in the malaise about politics and the disdain for government may also reflect the growth of dependence on government since the 1930s. Most people in the West, even those in the less statist United States, have come to rely on the state to solve most problems and to provide jobs, security for the aged, and medical care, as well as good schools. Socialism and communism may have collapsed, but heavy reliance on what Dahl describes as an increasingly complex and incomprehensible government has not. We expect much from the state, and we turn against elected officials because of their failure to accomplish what we want them to do. Ironically, the decline in confidence in government in a nation which suspects government, which does not want to rely on it, makes it more difficult for the political leaders to enact new programs and deal with problems that the public would like to see resolved, such as health care.

The Survival of the American Dream

Given the bad news about governance in the United States, what accounts for the continued stability of the American system? Why do we not witness grievous forms of mass unrest? Why is the major protest movement, that led by Ross Perot, basically centrist, even conservative with respect to economic and social policy? Part of the answer to the conundrum is that most Americans are not unhappy about their personal lives or prospects; if anything, the opposite is true. They still view the United States as a country that rewards personal integrity and hard work, as one that, government and politics apart, still works. The American Dream is still alive, even if the government and other institutions are seen as corrupt and inefficient. A 1994 survey-based study of "The American Dream" conducted for the Hudson Institute finds that over four-fifths, 81 percent, agree with the statement, "I am optimistic about my personal future," while about two-thirds, 64 percent, are "optimistic about America's future." Three-quarters, 74 percent, agreed that "In America, if you work hard, you can be anything you want to be." And almost 72 percent felt that "As Americans, we can always find a way to solve our problems and get what we want." And not surprisingly, when asked to choose between "having the opportunity to succeed" and "having security from failing," over three-quarters, 76 percent, opt for the former; only one-fifth, 20 percent, prefer the security option.

Gallup polling for *Times-Mirror* in 1994 presents similar results. Over two-thirds, 67 percent, expect their financial situation to improve a lot or some; only 14 percent say it will get worse. Large majorities reject the statement that "Success in life is pretty much determined by forces outside our control." Most affirm the traditional American laissez-faire ideology, with 88 percent agreeing with the statement "I admire people who get rich by working hard," and 85 percent agreeing that "Poor people have become too dependent on government assistance programs." More significantly, perhaps, 78 percent endorse the view: "The strength of this country today is mostly based on the success of American business."

The American political system, though distrusted and ineffective in dealing with major social issues, is clearly not in danger. Most Americans remain highly patriotic and religious, believe they are living in the best society in the world, and think that their country and economy, in spite of its problems, still offers them opportunity and economic security. Although the depression of the 1930s was worse here than in most of Europe, America came out of it with its party system, state institutions, and material values intact. The country will probably do the same today, although it must be acknowledged that the major parties appear somewhat more vulnerable than at any time since the Civil War.

American democracy is much less healthy now than at any time since World War II. Should we change our political institutions and move toward a parliamentary system? I must say no; in any case, it would be politically impossible and would undermine the legitimacy of our institutions. In addition, it should be noted that parliamentary systems such as in Canada, Britain, or Sweden do not seem to offer models of policy success either. And parliamentarism failed in most European countries in the period between the two World Wars and in post-World War II France.

Let me note, since this essay has been written for a meeting on the Americas, the criticisms of Juan Linz, Fred Riggs, and many others respecting the diffusion of the presidential divided authority system from the United States to Latin America. The critics argue that the presidential system, which combines the sources of authority (the head of state) and the agent of authority in one person and party, creates much more difficult problems of governance than occur in the other multi-party coalitional parliamentary systems. Such critics believe that parliamentary democracies, which permit power-sharing among competing groups, are better adapted to Latin American socio-political conditions. Adam Przeworski has presented comparative statistical data, drawn largely from Latin America, which suggest that parliamentary democracies have a somewhat greater longevity than presidential ones. A shift from presidential to parliamentary governance, while politically impossible for the United States, could take place in some Latin American countries, hopefully with positive outcomes.

Conclusion

Although many countries have recently taken up democracy, these new democracies have serious problems that raise questions of viability; there are also issues of governability, of overload, in most of the older established democracies, which are often held up as role models for the rest of the world. In particular, in the most important of these, the United States, democracy is much less healthy than it used to be. There has been a secular decline in political participation, in popular confidence in the political system and other major institutions, and in social trust and association, as well as a weakening of the voluntary institutions of civil society. On the other hand, television and other new technologies have arisen that appear to accentuate rather than offset the difficulties.

Crucial among civic institutions are the political parties. Their growing weakness, in combination with the inherent vulnerabilities of the internally conflicted American political system, are producing a state of governmental impotence, of "gridlock." Paradoxically, as government has become bigger, absorbing old institutions and taking on new roles, it has become less effective. Citizens feel (and are) more dependent on a government they trust less; and as a result of this distrust, government is less capable. Moreover, there is no clear direction for reform of our political institutions.

Finally, I would emphasize that Tocqueville was correct in placing more stress on the institutions of civil society than on government, and that therefore we should direct our attention to rebuilding associations and relationships that mediate between the state and citizenry.

References

Theodore Caplow, Howard M. Bahr, Bruce A. Chadwick, and John Modell, *Recent Social Trends in the United States, 1960-1990* (Frankfurt: Campus Verlag and Montreal: McGill University Press, 1990).

Committee for the Study of the American Electorate, "Primary Turnout Low GOP Gains, Democrats Lose, Low November Turnout Likely" (press release, Washington, D.C., September 23, 1994).

Robert Dahl, "The Ills of the System," *Dissent*, 40 (Fall 1993), 447-462.

E.J. Dionne, Jr., *Why American Hate Politics*. (New York: Touchstone Book, 1992 Second Edition).

The Hudson Institute, *The American Dream* (unpublished study, Indianapolis, 1994).

S.M. Lipset and William Schneider, *The Confidence Gap: Business, Labor and Government in the Public Mind* (Baltimore: Johns Hopkins University Press, expanded edition, 1987).

Thomas Mann and Norman Ornstein, eds., *Congress, the Press and the Public* (Washington, D.C.: American Enterprise Institute and Brookings Institution, 1994).

Norman Ornstein, "Less Seems More: What to Do About Contemporary Political Corruption," *The Responsive Community*, 4 (Winter 1993/94), 7-22.

Thomas E. Patterson, *Out of Order* (New York: Alfred A. Knopf, 1993).

Robert D. Putnam, "Bowling Alone: Democracy in America at the End of the Twentieth Century," (unpublished paper, Department of Government, Harvard University, August 1994).

William Schneider, "'Off With Their Heads': The Confidence Gap and the Revolt Against Professionalism in American Politics," in Gary Marks and Larry Diamond, eds., *Reexamining Democracy* (Newbury Park, CA: Sage Publications, 1993), 315-331.

The (Los Angeles) *Times-Mirror* Center, *The New Political Landscape* (Washington, D.C., 1994).

Chapter 2

Latin America: The Twisted Tree of Democracy

Beatrice Rangel Mantilla

During the so-called "lost decade of the 1980s," Latin America underwent its most profound political and economic revolution since Independence. It was during that decade that the Latin American people finally secured their full democratic rights after two centuries of relentless struggle. The institutions that had long restricted not only economic development but the entire nature of political participation were destroyed.

The misnamed "Latin American economic crisis" was a crisis of political power initially expressed in economic terms. This process of political transformation coincided with and indeed was rooted in an acute economic crisis. The latter made feasible the macroeconomic adjustment and opening toward the world economy, which created conditions for the present boom. To call this period of transformations a "lost decade" muddles the analysis of these countries' future potential and obscures the transformation of the very institutions that quashed democracy and inhibited the development of market forces in the past.

During our two centuries of independence, we never escaped from two legacies of Spanish colonialism. These legacies produced economic and political structures markedly different from those of the United States in the same period. And that is why these structures collapsed so suddenly in the face of the pressures created by technological change and economic globalization.

The institutional framework of power relationships in Latin America is the primary product of the logic of Spanish colonization, which was to extract precious metals to underpin its policies of economic mercantilism. But imperial Spain was also interested in reinforcing its status as a major European power by drawing on support from the papacy. For this purpose the Spanish crown guaranteed the expansion of the Roman Catholic faith in its recently discovered overseas territories, thus transplanting authoritarian institutions to virgin lands. Even then, Spain was economically and politically backward compared to countries such as England (which was already laying the foundations of the Industrial Revolution) or the Italian city-states (great practitioners of commerce

Translated by Mark Falcoff.

and republicanism). Thus, Spain's political, economic, and ideological back-wardness in the metropolis combined with a mercantile economic policy and the exportation of centralized, bureaucratic institutions. It is easy to see why Latin America's own institutional framework greatly inhibited its development toward democracy and free markets. Indeed, democracy and market economy are two dimensions of the same historical project, to find ways of creating wealth and regulating relations between the individual and society that guarantee and enrich individual liberties.

The historical consequence of the crisis of the 1980s was the rupturing of the old post-colonial institutional framework. In effect, the economic collapse produced by the exhaustion of the import-substitution model meant the end of an entire historical era marked by vigorous state intervention in the economy. That intervention was designed not so much to promote growth as it was to sustain a political model based on clientelism. This political economy based itself purely on the redistribution of income extracted by the state from productive sectors. Thus,the well-being of most individuals or groups depended wholly on their proximity to power, to those who controlled the state. This was a quasi-corporativist alliance, whose principal objective was to maintain stability through complicated pacts and arrangements between the state and representatives of different social sectors. Such a mode of government prevented the growth of genuine democratic participation in Latin America.

This kind of state collapsed under the weight of external and internal contradictions. As a consequence of urbanization and technological devel-opment, society became too diversified for management by a centralized state. Moreover, the consolidation of oligopolistic or monopolistic econo-mies slowed down rates of growth. Government revenues soon fell far below the level required simply to maintain a heavy, centralized government apparatus. Finally, state intervention in areas best left to private enterprise eventually robbed it of the capacity to achieve the government's proper objectives — security and defense, public health and education, and the administration of justice.

To these contradictions and failures, the development of new means of communication added new civic pressures. Soon a tele-educated public was comparing its own to more advanced societies. All of this became explosive when the traditional economic base of our polity began to erode as the advanced countries initiated processes of industrial reconversion. The Latin American countries could no longer comfortably rely upon revenue from the export of raw materials. That was when the anachronistic institutional order inherited from colonialism collapsed. Thanks to that painful but ultimately liberating event, today Latin America is advantageously placed to construct democratic institutions that are economically self-sustaining.

Different Roads to Democracy

Though culturally, linguistically, and ethnically similar, each of the Latin American nations is building unique democratic institutions, responding to specific geographical, economic, and social factors.

In general, the political transformations achieved since the 1980s have varied largely in accordance with the ways in which the old clientelistic institutions were overturned. In Argentina, for example, the authoritarian populism of the military regime (1976-1982) was dismantled by defeat on the battlefield. In Central America, democracy has been the product of social pressures and civil wars that eventually reached an impasse. In Brazil, the transition from dictatorship to democracy followed Brazil's historic pattern, whereby change is effected by an agreement among elites. In contrast, Venezuelan democratic stability was based on clientelistic redistribution and huge petroleum receipts, so that when world oil prices collapsed, Venezuela's economy and government were affected dramatically.

Mexico displays yet another pattern. Economic transformations have succeeded in opening the way to political pluralism, allowing new political actors to enter the scene. In Chile, democracy was achieved after an economic boom transferred power to the middle classes.

All these processes, nonetheless, have a common characteristic: their final objective is to dismantle the unwieldy apparatus of government, which only guaranteed stability at the high cost of inhibiting true political participation. In fact, none of these traditional structures would have survived the current climate of economic competition with the accompanying need to incorporate entire populations into productive activities.

None of these roads taken by Latin American countries replicate the path to democracy taken by the United States, but their final products are just as valid as U.S. democracy. Even in problematic situations such as Venezuela's, once the society grasps that past rules can no longer be maintained, the democratic system will be reinforced within a new institutional framework — one that is genuinely pluralistic and competitive. In truth, the scant popular support given to the two recent military conspiracies reflects more than anything else the Venezuelan people's readiness for and belief in democracy.

Storms Behind Us: The New Hemispheric Project

This heterogeneity and the lack of a theoretical consensus have led some analysts to predict that in time the pendulum will swing back, and Latin America will return to various forms of authoritarianism. Such predictions are, I believe, ill-founded. In the first place, economic openings and genuine competition virtually guarantee the continued emergence of new groups that will participate in decision making. In turn, competition will cause ordinary citizens to expect continued economic progress and raise the price of institutional rupture to prohibitive levels. As people realize that opportunities for social and economic improvement are based upon their own initiatives, a genuine middle-class culture — the foundation of democratic stability — will be created.

Second, the processes of regional integration that are underway are bound to produce dramatic economic growth over the next decade and have already raised expectations. Indeed, the most conservative estimates anticipate a 7 percent growth for the years 1995-2000 for the member countries of the Southern Common Market (MERCOSUR), Argentina, Brazil, Uruguay and Paraguay. The members of the North American Free Trade Agreement (NAFTA), Canada, the

United States, and Mexico, are expected to reach a 5 percent growth rate for the same period. Except for Nicaragua, the Central American countries have already achieved this level.[1] The English-speaking Caribbean countries are beginning to feel the effects of South American economic integration. The vigorous growth of Colombia, Ecuador, and Peru will eventually create opportunities for stabilization and growth in Venezuela. Chile already boasts more than a decade of high growth rates, and it is the only country in the hemisphere whose internal savings rate reaches 20 percent per year.

Third, it is obvious that optimism and confidence in the future have suddenly taken hold in Latin America, particularly among ordinary citizens. A cursory glance at the front pages of the thirteen most important newspapers of the region reveals that — with the exception of Venezuela — 60 percent of the space deals with news about new development goals, achievements of integration, increases in the value of national assets, the opening of new businesses, the presence of intermediate bodies apart from traditional parties, and so forth.[2] Contrast this with the front pages of the ten principal dailies of the United States, filled with citizens' unhappiness with foreign policy, public services, physical safety, and the quality of political leadership.

Fourth, Latin American values are changing. We are eagerly embracing modernity. Nationalist sentiments, suspicions about the outside world, as well as doubts about our own capacities are disappearing. In their place we see a growth of self-confidence and a desire to change. Such sentiments find varied expressions. In politics, an examination of parliaments in a dozen Latin American nations over the last ten years reveals interesting data. More than half of those currently sitting have replaced incumbents of long standing. Many of the newcomers have gained national significance by organizing their communities. Equally important changes have taken place at the presidential level. Except for Colombia, Chile, Mexico, Paraguay, and Venezuela, no political party has proved capable of winning two consecutive presidencies. In the last fifteen years, the percentage of voters in each election has grown (in contrast to the United States, where it has decreased).

In the cultural area, surveys by American companies in Latin America to discover consumer tastes reveal that England and France, once the models for Latin America, have been replaced by the United States, Chile, and Argentina.

New institutional developments are preventing any one force from monopolizing political participation. In many countries the key is decentralization. Reduced powers and jurisdictions of central governments mean that local communities are acquiring decision-making power. With that, the capacity of the ordinary citizen to define and limit the scope of the authorities is growing. The success of decentralization is evident, among other signs, in the growth of civic and non-governmental organizations. According to the Organization of American States, the number of such grass-roots groups has quintupled in the last five years.[3]

Programs of social development, such as that undertaken by former President Carlos Salinas de Gortari in Mexico under the name of "Solidarity" have increased the power of local communities even more, by stimulating their participation in the use of public resources to solve their problems. The terrain won by these communities in the area of self-government will be difficult to wrest back from them by a mere swing of the political pendulum — that is, a reversion back to authoritarianism. Let us recall that authoritarian solutions are the product of a crisis of legitimacy, something which surely will not exist when democracy is effectively exercised by a majority of the citizens.

The fiscal equilibrium achieved by policies of economic adjustment and economic opening is another factor that reinforces stability. The state can now maintain itself only by collecting taxes. This, in turn, allows Latin American citizens to exercise new, previously unheard-of powers to influence the state. These new powers to the people should curb authoritarian temptations.

Finally, the development of the mass media provides ordinary Latin Americans with a new way to restrain authority: information about the actual conduct of government business. Now that the media has been freed from the limitations imposed by the clientelistic state and with the development of satellite communications, governments can no longer conceal their behavior. Today all elected officials know that at the end of their terms they must confront an electorate stimulated and informed by the news media. Therefore, officials are inclined to be more efficient and accountable to their constituents. Better levels of information also translate into a greater selectivity on the part of the electorate, which in turn reinforces better performance in office.

While there are still important tasks ahead — particularly a profound reform of judicial systems — as well as the need for continued economic growth, the historic path chosen by the Latin American nations these last ten years affords more optimism than doubts about its permanence and durability.

The final years of the twentieth century present an unusual challenge to the countries of the Western Hemisphere: to construct an economic community capable of responding efficiently to the demands of a world economy and an international system gradually evolving toward multipolarity. If the hemisphere does not make the intellectual effort to understand the unique aspects of the Latin American transformations and to act within parameters appropriate to them, it will confront serious limitations to economic integration and democratic consolidation. Let us recall Sir Isaiah Berlin's advice in *The Twisted Tree of Humanity*: the human race is capable of following the most torturous routes to free institutions. To fix a linear course for the development of democracy in this region, as indeed in any other, would be a useless exercise.

Notes

1. Inter-American Development Bank, "Economic and Social Progress in Latin America and The Caribbean 1994." The IDB estimates growth rates for Central America during 1994 to be: Costa Rica, 6.1 percent; El Salvador, 5 percent; Guatemala, 4.9 percent; Honduras, 0.5 percent; and Nicaragua, -1 percent. Except for Nicaragua, all remaining economies in Central America are undergoing expansionary trends. Honduras' poor performance during 1994 is atypical, for it was the result of extraordinarily severe weather conditions. Indeed, the combined impact of the tropical storm "Gert" and the drought that affected the Central and Northeastern regions of the country destroyed over half of the Honduran agricultural product. Expansionary trends, however, are clearly present in the Honduran economy. The proportion of gross domestic product attributable to fisheries increased 40 percent over the last years, while assembling activities grew by 30 percent. Industrial domestic product maintained its growth momentum by sustaining a 3.7 percent rate. Nicaragua, on the contrary, does not show signs of reactivation for 1994. Forecasts for 1995-1999 for Nicaragua are not favorable either.

2. The newspapers reviewed for Latin America were *El Excelsior* (Mexico); *El Tiempo* (Bogotá); *El Nacional* (Caracas); *The Nation* (Bridgetown); *El Comercio* (Lima); *El Mercurio* (Santiago); *Clarín* (Buenos Aires); *O Globo* (Rio de Janeiro); *Folha* (São Paulo); *Listín Diario* (República Dominicana); *El Comercio* (Quito); *The Starbroek News* (Georgetown); *The Gleaner* (Kingston). For the United States, the newspapers were *The New York Times, The Wall Street Journal, The Boston Globe, The Christian Science Monitor, The Washington Post, The Los Angeles Times, The Miami Herald, The Chicago Tribune, The Minneapolis Star,* and *The Houston Chronicle.*

3. Interamerican Institute of Human Rights, *Annual Report 1993*, San José, Costa Rica.

Chapter 3

Democracy and Citizenship in Contemporary Latin America

Manuel Mora y Araujo

"Americans seem to have lost the broader sense of politics that goes beyond what governments do. They have lost the names for what citizens do (David Matthews, *Politics for People*)."

Since the 1980s, political changes have been taking place in Latin American countries along lines similar to those which have become familiar in much of the world. Ours is an epoch of democratic consolidation, and we are seeing enormous changes in the political life of our nations. The most visible aspects of this trend are the following:

- The establishment of legitimate democratic regimes.
- Economic reform in the direction of fiscal stability and market economies, accompanied generally by strong popular support.
- Demand for major changes in "political style."
- The tendency to resolve endemic conflicts through peaceful means.

However, at the same time that such policies are gaining ground and becoming part of the consciousness of the Latin American citizenries, a noticeable climate of distrust of existing institutions has also emerged. This lack of confidence does not exhibit the same features that it did in the past: contempt for democratic principles and the constant search for coalitions capable of mounting a coup d'état. Rather, the prevailing attitude among Latin Americans is one of indifference toward politics and lack of interest in civic affairs.

This climate of distrust manifests itself as:

- Prevalent public concern about corruption;
- Loss of credibility of heads of state, often culminating in impeachments, forced resignations, or defeat within a constitutional framework;
- The discrediting of government institutions — executive as well as legislative and judicial;
- Widespread political apathy, especially among the young.

Translated by Erick Bridoux and Robert S. Leiken.

How can these two tendencies, democratic stability and lack of faith in democratic institutions, be explained? I believe that seemingly ambivalent attitudes toward the democratic process result from the contrast between the slow, often obscure transformation of political institutions and the speed with which changes are taking place in society, particularly in regard to the technological infrastructure and the evolving attitudes of the population. This difference in timing implies a challenge to find new forms of institutional legitimation. Old institutions have reduced the efficacy of political representation and alienated common citizens from the political process in their communities.

Our societies wish to accelerate the process of adapting political institutions to the realities of the contemporary world. However, this process generates tensions that often are perceived as threats to the democratic order.

Political Transformation

The transformations demanded by contemporary democracy affect many aspects of political life. These include forms of representation, leadership style, decision-making procedures, the structures through which interests are articulated, and the selection of leaders — in brief, political parties. The traditional model of interaction between political leaders and the citizenry, which was based on the mediation of party mechanisms, has become obsolete, as present-day communications and information render such mediation unnecessary.

Also outdated is the customary Latin American leadership style — based on the providential attributes of the leaders and on an asymmetric, unidirectional mode of communication. Today's media facilitate symmetric, interactive communications.

In the democratic political tradition to date, leaders made the most important policy decisions according to their own lights, subject only to the most restricted outside influences. In a sense, democracy was based on the popular legitimacy of the top policy maker rather than on the policies themselves. A new conception of democracy is now gaining ground, one that demands greater popular participation in decision making and increased accountability from leaders.

The traditional ways in which political parties articulated interests and selected leaders within structures closed to popular participation have been exhausted. By definition, political parties are programmatic and divisive. Today, there is a growing popular tendency to transcend party loyalties and look for consensus on specific issues. Furthermore, the nomination of leaders within closed, programmatic, divisive party structures — usually through a *cursus honorum* controlled by the party bosses — no longer produces leaders who actually represent the people.

Society and Political Culture

These changes have their roots in the social infrastructure within the political culture. Society's infrastructure is changing as a result of the increased globalization of the world, expansion of communication, the lower cost and increased access of information, the more active role of the media, and the diffusion of public opinion surveys.

At the same time, major changes are also taking place in the political culture. The political culture of conflict is giving way to one based on consensus. The elements that unite the various segments of the body politic are now considered more important than the divisive elements. The culture of political intolerance is giving way to one of tolerance. Latin Americans now believe less in absolute truths and more in truths that are built gradually by comparing and synthesizing different points of view.

The personalist, providential, charismatic leaders of the past, considered supermen, are being replaced by leaders who see themselves as *primus inter pares* seeking specific solutions to specific problems. The old notion that governability depends on the absolute power of the leader is now yielding to the idea of limited and shared power.

Political parties, once considered the fundamental element of democratic order, are increasingly viewed as obstructions of democracy. Political parties will be difficult to discard since no structures have emerged to replace the parties' functions. Nevertheless, the growing consensus is that "political parties are the problem rather than the solution."

Legitimacy, Governability, and Participation

These changes raise fundamental questions but provide no clearcut answers. Do these changes threaten fundamental democratic principles? Are the values that sustain democracy being extended and deepened, or are they simply changing, eventually to be replaced by other values?

The systematic analyses of data from various public opinion surveys in various Latin American countries lead to reflections that together may form a reasonably sound hypothesis. In my view, the basic values of democracy — representative government, equality before the law, limited power — are not being questioned in Latin America. However, the traditional ways in which these values have been expressed and defended are being scrutinized very critically. To phrase it differently, these basic values must be reconciled and combined with other political values that manifest a new pragmatism.

The priority in present-day democracies is governability, which in practical terms means executive efficacy, the capacity to resolve problems that society defines as serious. We must not forget that the current Latin American democracies are the products of previous failed military governments, whose sole source of legitimacy was the capacity to govern increasingly ungovernable societies.

In the present political context, Latin American societies seek, actively I would say, to limit the power of the state. These limitations appear to be based more on the vigor of political pluralism than on an effective judiciary (which in many cases means that judicial reform remains pending). Pluralism, in turn, is based on freedom of the press and the unrestrained diffusion of information — above all on public opinion surveys that reduce "pluralist ignorance" and oblige political leaders to accept the reality that information flows in two directions.

The legitimacy of contemporary democracies can be formulated as follows: governability + participation + leadership.

Economic Realities

One of the relatively new traits exhibited by the current democratic process in Latin America is the massive acceptance of orthodox economic policies, the principal objectives of which are inflation control, fiscal stability, and deregulation of the economy. To the surprise of many observers — accustomed to believe and to argue that such policies could only be implemented by military governments backed by the power of international financial institutions — economic orthodoxy now helps to win elections and, in many cases, buttresses political support among the least privileged social sectors.

The new economic orthodoxy is producing a new type of economic development, with decisive participation of foreign capital, more open economies, and increased microeconomic competitiveness. However, these new economic processes are creating along with economic growth — often at high rates — greater distributive inequalities, which, in turn, generate new social cleavages that do not relate to old class stratifications.

Typically, our societies are separated into three segments: 1) those who welcome the new economic models, 2) those who resist them or are unable to adapt accordingly, and 3) those who only passively accept them. These three segments of society — those who welcome, resist, or passively accept economic orthodoxy — do not correspond to traditional strata defined in accordance with income levels and living standards. Those who support the evolution of traditional structures into market-driven economies come from both the most affluent and the poorest members of society, and the same is true regarding those who resist these changes.

The overarching political consequence of this situation is the end of class politics as we have known it. Political coalitions are increasingly formed on the basis of other criteria, with political leaders enjoying a larger measure of autonomy while facing more demanding challenges, both in regard to elections and the exercise of governmental authority.

The Public Agenda

The issues in Latin American public opinion agendas are broadly similar and, in any event, share one major concern: the preoccupation with past failures. In societies that have suffered high rates of inflation, the top priority is an economic policy capable of controlling the inflationary spiral. In societies that have been ravaged by conflict, the priority is to achieve peace through negotiation. Economic stability combined with social peace is the best formula for electoral success, as demonstrated in Central America, Argentina, Peru, and, most recently, Brazil.

Together with economic matters, issues such as corruption and electoral reform have recently risen to the top of the agenda in many countries. Citizens demand new regulations designed to curtail the ability of members of the political elite to obtain illicit benefits and from perpetuating themselves in power.

Likewise a comparative analysis of public opinion surveys conducted in different countries reveals notable similarities among the public images of social groups. In general, the productive sector is highly respected, while public regard for the distributive sector (labor unions) and government institutions (parties, legislatures, the judiciary) is clearly in decline.

The "capitalist model" is no longer taboo, and in many Latin American societies foreign investment is welcomed by the bulk of the population. However, there is often widespread suspicion about the actual entrepreneurs whom people know personally; frequently the public views them as more interested in immediate profits than in the long-term welfare of their communities.

The New Mediations: Press and Public Opinion Polls

Among the many elements that make up the fabric of the new democracies in the continent, the media and public opinion surveys have played particularly significant roles.

Significant aspects of the role previously played by political parties, such as mediating structures between leaders and masses, are played today by the media, as they disseminate information, create public opinion, and provide entertainment. As a consequence, politics has been divested of its "sacred" aura. Indeed, the media works today, quite often, to convert politics into yet another form of entertainment. In this capacity, the media connect apolitical citizens to the world of politics, albeit from a position that demands little or no active involvement. But the media are also a vehicle for the two-way flow of information and, perhaps as no other factor, constitute the principal source of restriction on the conduct of officials. In this regard, freedom of the press — something not always so appreciated by Latin Americans in the past — has now become one of the most cherished values in the new democracies.

Public opinion surveys also have acquired a central role in the last few years because they perform two different functions, each having introduced new elements into politics. As a strategic resource in election campaigns, they introduce the tools of the market into the political trade. To some degree, they transform the candidate into a consumer item, and allow the search for votes to be approached in the same way as the search for customers.

As a public information resource, on the other hand, opinion polls democratize political decisions perhaps as no other institution can: they make citizens' preferences and evaluations transparent and objective, while destroying the virtual monopoly of information once held by political parties and their leaders. In this sense, opinion surveys contribute enormously to placing the independent citizen at the center of the political process, upgrading the popular agenda in relation to that of the leaders.

The impact of the media and public opinion polls can be clearly seen in electoral campaigns. Traditionally, campaigns consisted of the mobilization of party militants and individuals with strong political convictions. As a rule, the candidate and his followers gathered en masse to communicate nothing but slogans and chants, characterized by expressions of contempt for the opposition and other non-participant sectors. Now political campaigns are marketing tools used to attract independent voters. Far from communicating with their loyal followers in rallies, candidates now try to keep them hidden, while approaching non-partisan citizens as their equals. In most cases, the image of the candidate speaking exaltedly from the heights of a podium to his fanatical followers has given way to that of a candidate walking the streets, speaking little and listening intently to those who, on occasion, choose to speak with him.

A New Culture

It is not an exaggeration to regard these profound political and economic changes occurring at the bedrock of current democratic regimes as the basis for a new civic culture. Some of the specific processes that have unfolded during the last few years on our continent suggest that the new civic culture is engendering new expectations from the political system:

- Citizens have accepted strong budgetary restrictions on the state, although they also expect more governmental sensitivity to the needs of the community and more efficiency in public spending.

- People have generally accepted the model of the private economy, but they also demand more responsibility on the part of the leadership of both the public and the private sectors.

- Citizens are trying to play more important roles in politics through new channels of participation. This includes not only a demand for greater utilization of the plebiscite, but also the creation of new spaces for public debate in which voluntary civic associations increasingly play a larger role than political parties. These new expectations reveal a public perception that the selection of public representatives must take place in accordance with new guidelines.

It often seems as if the new Latin American civic culture is too effervescent, frequently overwhelming institutional channels and the capabilities of the political leadership. Indeed, the lack of faith in existing institutions can be explained by the fact that, in many cases, there is less leadership.

However, these changes — despite the difficulties and tensions that they inevitably generate — are causes for optimism regarding the political future of our societies. We cannot yet be certain about reaching an equilibrium point, if it exists, that will signal that the new forms of democracy currently under development have become consolidated. However, we can suggest that this point will be associated with the adoption of civic and human values higher than those of the political culture of personalism, intolerance, violence, and non-accountability.

I sense that we are achieving a style of democratic political life in which the citizen counts more and the responses to major social problems are increasingly generated through a process of interaction between the leaders and the led.

Chapter 4

Democracy and Populism

Harvey C. Mansfield

The success of the American Constitution is often remarked but hardly ever explained. Since it is easy to make a constitution, most people assume that the difficulty lies in getting it obeyed. How can the power of government be restrained? How can the elites be prevented from taking advantage of their positions? These are the usual questions, and the usual answer is that a constitution will be obeyed if it brings more democracy.

But what happens when democracy comes to power? Are there any dangers it can bring? Once democracy is established, the gravest danger may arise not from outside but from within democracy. That was the belief of the American founders. The constitution they made may well owe its success to the attention they gave to the danger they saw as intrinsic to democracy. James Madison called it "majority faction" (Federalist 10).

Making a constitution is easy, but making one well is not. It is easy for supporters of democracy to see the advantages of democracy and to assert them against the reactionary regimes that democracy replaces. It is not so easy for democrats to see the vices of democracy or, if they do see them, to face them and deal with them. Most difficult of all is to find democratic remedies for the ills of democracy. This the American founders did for their constitution, and I believe that is the reason for its success. The American Constitution, one could say, is the main source of its own success. It has generated and sustained its own support by encouraging constitutional behavior in both the government and the people.

What Madison called majority faction is known today as populism. "Populist" and "popular" are often used interchangeably, but the difference is fundamental. "Popular" is what the people want, but "populist" is giving the people what they want through adventitious means outside the constitution.

Populism is, of course, nothing new in American politics, and it takes many forms. The first to be called populists arose over a century ago in a mainly rural movement directed against cities, corporations, and the educated. Soon they were absorbed into the Progressive movement, which introduced such populist measures as referenda and party primaries, whereby the people bypass legislatures and party organizations to accomplish their will. Parties themselves, though now considered part of the

27

established structure even if not part of the constitution, were once populist means for revitalizing the constitution (when Thomas Jefferson first organized the Democratic Party in order to win the election of 1800).

The activists of the late 1960s were educated populists who goaded the Establishment with demands for "power to the people." They might be called populists of the left. But currently in America, populism has been taken up by conservatives in referenda proposals for tax limitation and term limits and in constitutional amendments for school prayer and the balanced budget. Much conservative populism is directed against judicial activism by the Supreme Court. Judicial activism is itself a form of populism carried out by a constitutional branch when it is dissatisfied with lack of progress in other sectors of government.

Still another form of populism comes from outside politics — from the new technology of the media. A free press allows communication between the people and the government but also requires the people to read and think (to a degree). Radio is more intimate than the press; television, even more so. Television provides less information and more entertainment. It makes its viewers intolerant of boredom and then fears to bore them; altogether, they become less capable as democratic citizens.

Public opinion polls are another extra-political form of populism. Polls were originally intended merely to predict how people would vote in elections. Now they de-legitimize elections because they show more promptly what the people want regardless of whom they voted for. Instead of asking, as in elections, who should be entrusted with government and for what ends, polls often ask the people what they want at that moment. Polls tell governments just how popular (or unpopular) they are at every moment, so that they become subject more and more to temporary shifts in opinion. Worse, governments begin to confuse popularity with policy.

The desultory means of populism are distinct from the constitutional method of registering what the people want — in elections. The various forms of populism share a common spirit of impatience, of a people fed up with the usual ways and ready to try something new. No doubt they represent a generic force endemic to American democracy, even to all modern democracy. As Alexis de Tocqueville reminded us, our democracy is constantly in process of democratizing itself further. Democracy in its populist mood tends to become impatient with constitutional forms and institutions, regarding them as barriers between the people and the government. It wants government to react more promptly and surely to popular will.

The difference between populism and constitutional democracy corresponds to the distinction Madison drew between a democracy and a republic. What Madison called democracy, we would call "pure democracy," where the people rule directly rather than through their representatives. Madison (and the other founders) considered such a regime suitable only for small cities but not for modern states. On the basis of historical study, Madison concluded that such democracies were vulnerable to demagogues and characterized by cataclysmic shifts from anarchy to tyranny.[1] A new kind of republic was needed, one not subject to the flaws of "pure" democracy. So the American founders undertook to make a constitution after a critical and introspective view of previous republics. They did not trust that simply by adopting democracy their problems would be solved. Their wisdom is still a guide for us today, because the threat of populism is the lasting demon of popular government.

The constitutional connection between government and people is formed by elections. We should beware of nonelective forms of representation that reduce the importance of elections. An election leaves a space between government and people even as it connects them. Far from being a defect, this is a central virtue of elections. A politician is elected to an office with constitutionally or legally defined powers and for a definite term. The powers give him scope to act between elections so as to build a record during his term. If he is an executive, he can perform two very different functions: react quickly in an emergency and carry out long-term plans. In the first case, he need not fear temporary unpopularity; in the second, he can work over time to win popular opinion to his side.

A legislator, though he may reflect shifting opinion rather more, has, nonetheless, the opportunity with his office (and through the complicated network of committees) to deliberate alone and with others about what should be done. That is how the "cool and deliberate sense of the community," as Madison called it, comes into play. One meaning of "deliberate" is slow; another is careful and reasonable. When people are in haste, their reason usually does not operate well. With a well-made constitution, a democratic people can curb their mercurial tendencies and restrain their impulsive demands for action. Such pressures characterize democracy wherever it is practiced; they are not peculiar to certain races, cultures, or temperaments. The task of constitutional government is to deal with them prudently, neither suppressing nor endorsing them.

The advantage of constitutional space for the people is a certain detachment from the government which enables them to judge the government. If the government reacts too faithfully to popular will, the people get too close to evaluate it. Instead of being their government, the government is the people, and they have no one to blame but themselves. A general distrust of politicians can be healthy to a democracy, but it can also be an evasion of responsibility. Democratic governments need responsible citizens as much as they need honest politicians.

Constitutional space is the genius of American democracy. It enables a popular government to do unpopular things when necessary, while at the same time providing for the people's verdict in due course. Constitutional distance is a democratic remedy for democracy's ills because it gets the best out of a democratic people — the best leaders and the best collective judgment on them. Constitutional space does not guarantee success in government, but it affords the best chance.

Populism with all its devices for popularity has not made democratic government more popular. On the contrary, populism undermines democratic legitimacy by making the government timid and the people impatient. I do not mean that it is always wrong to make a democracy more democratic (as we have seen, political parties were a populist and extra-constitutional means of advancing constitutional democracy). But democracy needs a constitution to save itself from the seductions of populism. The purpose of a constitution is not to thwart the people's will but, just the contrary, to fulfill it.

Note

---

1. See *The Federalist,* 9,10, 14 and also see the argument by Montesquieu that presents the defects of the virtuous republics of the Classical era: *The Spirit of the Laws,* 4.7, 8; 5, 6; 6.9; 7, 10; 8.2; 9.1; 11.4.

Chapter 5

The Loss of Civil Society and the Decline of Liberal Democratic Faith

Jean Bethke Elshtain

Liberal democracy is in trouble in America. Experts and ordinary citizens lament the growth of a culture of mistrust, cynicism, and scandal. Although a dwindling band of pundits and apologists insist that Americans are suffering the pangs of dislocation en route to salutary change, even progress, such reassurances ring increasingly hollow. The evidence indicates a growth of corrosive forms of isolation, boredom, and despair, declining levels of involvement in politics from simple acts such as the vote to more demanding participation in political parties and local, civic associations, an overall weakening, in other words, of democratic civil society.

Social scientists who have investigated the sharp decline in participation argue that the evidence points to nothing less than a crisis in "social capital formation," the forging of bonds of social and political trust and competence.[1] The pernicious effects of rising mistrust, privatization, and anomie are many. For example, there is empirical support for the popularly held view that where neighborhoods are intact, drug and alcohol abuse, crime, and truancy among the young diminish. Because neighborhoods are less and less likely to be intact, all forms of socially destructive behavior are on the rise. Americans at the end of the twentieth century suffer from the effects of a dramatic decline in the formation of social bonds, networks, and trust coupled with a diminution in investment in children. Children, in particular, have borne the brunt of negative social trends. All one need do is look at any American newspaper any day of the week to learn about the devastating effects on the young. Family breakdown generates unparented children who attend schools that increasingly resemble detention homes rather than centers of enduring training, discipline, and education and contributes to out-of-wedlock births and violence at unprecedented levels.[2]

Democratic theorists historically have either taken for granted a backdrop of vibrant, informal and formal civic associations, or they have articulated explicitly the relationship between democracy and the everyday actions and spirit of a people. Democracy requires laws, constitutions, and authoritative institutions but also depends on democratic dispositions. These include a preparedness to work with others for shared ends, a combination of often strong convictions coupled with a readiness to compromise in the recognition that one can't always get everything one wants, a sense of individuality and a commitment to civic goods that are not the possession of one person or of one small group alone. The world that nourished and sustained such democratic dispositions was a thickly interwoven social fabric — the web of mediating institutions already noted.

Tocqueville, in *Democracy in America,* warned of a world different from the robust democracy he surveyed. He urged Americans to take to heart a possible corruption of their way of life. In his worst-case scenario, narrowly self-involved individualists, disarticulated from the saving constraints and nurture of overlapping associations of social life, would require more and more controls "from above" to muffle at least somewhat the disintegrative effects of egoism. To this end, civic spaces between citizens and the state needed to be secured and nourished. Only many small-scale civic bodies would enable citizens to cultivate democratic virtues and to play an active role in the democratic community. Tocqueville's fears were not that anarchy would result but, rather, that new forms of domination might arise. With the disintegration of all social webs, the individual would find himself or herself isolated and impotent, exposed and unprotected. Into this power vacuum would move a centralized, top-heavy state or other centralized and organized forces that would, so to speak, push social life to the lowest common denominator.

A recent *New York Times* article on the 1994 campaign reports that "U.S. Voters Focus on Selves, Poll Says." The article raises questions about the long-range impact of such attitudes on the legitimacy and sustainability of liberal democratic institutions. The *Times* noted a "turn inward" and the lack of any "clear direction in the public's political thinking other than frustration with the current system and an eager responsiveness to alternative political solutions and appeals."[3] Based on a *Times-Mirror* survey, the article noted that manifestations of voter frustration included growing disidentification with either of the major parties and massive political rootlessness among the young tethered to high rates of pessimism about the future. Most striking was a significant decline in "public support for social welfare programs," although the level of social tolerance for minorities and homosexuals was high so long as one did not have to bear the burden of financial support or direct "hands-on" involvement in the issue.[4]

The Spiral of Delegitimation

Two trends are traceable directly to the collapse of America's social ecology or, alternatively, helped to bring about the negative developments reported in the *Times-Mirror* survey. One is the tendency to remove political disputation from the political arena into the courts. Thus, Americans have witnessed over the past four decades a tendency to derail public debate by judicial fiat. The second is the emergence of a new form of plebiscitary democracy that reduces voters and legislators alike to passive (albeit angry) consumers or instruments. It is not overstating the case to speak of a "spiral of delegitimation" that has its origins in widespread cynicism about government and politics, the disintegration of civil society, a pervasive sense of powerlessness, and other cultural phenomena.

The political scientist James Q. Wilson argues that one reason Americans are more cynical and less trusting than they used to be is that government increasingly has taken on issues that it is ill-equipped to handle well — volatile moral questions such as abortion and "family values," for example. These "wedge issues," as political strategists call them, were generated in part by federal courts who made decisions in the 1960s and 1970s on a whole range of cultural questions without due consideration of how public support for juridically mandated outcomes might be generated. Such juridical moves not only froze out citizen debate but deepened a juridical model of politics, first pushed by liberal activists but now embraced by their conservative counterparts. Juridical politics is "winner take all" built on an adversarial model. This model, in turn, spurs "direct mail" and other mass membership organizations whose primary goal is to give no quarter in any matter of direct interest to them and to them alone. By guaranteeing that the forces on either side of such issues as abortion, or certain highly controversial mandated "remedies" to enforce racial or gender equity, need never debate directly with each other through deliberate processes and legislatures, the courts deepened citizen frustration and fueled a politics of resentment.

In turn, this politics of resentment tends to reduce legislators to passive instruments of single-issue lobbies and medial overkill. That is, even as judicial overreach takes issues out of the hands of citizens and legislators, it also appears to be one more factor eroding the deliberative functions of the legislative branch. Take, for example, the continuing American travail over the politics of abortion. One begins with a deeply contentious matter on which people of good will are divided. The Supreme Court makes a dramatic preemptory move (Roe v. Wade, 1973) that undercuts a nationwide political debate that had grown up from the grass roots. Sixteen states had already moved to make abortion more widely available, and others were poised to take up the question. The Supreme Court's action aroused strong and shocked opposition. The debate turned immediately into a harsh "for" or "against" politics that generated direct-mail, single-issue membership groups who vowed to evaluate representatives on the basis of abortion. But, in a way, this was a desperate strategy as all post-Roe politics had to make its way to the Court, the Court having taken over final prerogative on the question. This model of juridical preemption followed by resentment at the outcome, or fear on the part of those who support it that a mandated outcome may be reversed, frames political questions in a way that places them "beyond compromise."

In the face of such developments, aggrieved citizens, say, in effect, "let's take things back," through direct, rather than representative democracy. Indeed, the *Times-Mirror* survey cited above concluded that the "Perot phenomenon" that speaks to widespread voter anger and resentment went deeper and was more persistent than experts believed. It comes down to this: Judicial fiat displaces institutions of constitutional democracy by radically expanding its own mandate into the realm of democratic debate and compromise where things can be worked out in a rough and ready way. In turn, the proclaimed solution to expanded juridical power, plebiscitary or direct democracy, poses a threat of another (albeit related) sort by promoting the illusion that the unmediated "will of the people" will have final say on all issues. Although we are nowhere close to an official plebiscitary system, the trend is disturbing.

Taken together, the tendency to govern by polls (word has it that the current and several previous administrations bring pollsters to high-level strategy meetings in order to decide what policy should be), the craven capitulation to threats from such mass membership organizations as the American Association of Retired People (AARP) or the National Rifle Association (NRA), and the rise of a very sour populism that feeds on mistrust of government and hatred of politicians — all these excite plebiscitary fervor that deepens the spiral of delegitimation. Currently, those who call themselves populists target anyone unlucky enough to hold government office. Advocates of direct democracy claim that they will perfect democracy by eliminating all barriers between the people's will and its forthright articulation. An elected representative is no longer viewed as someone designated to study and to weigh issues; rather, he or she is to be instructed and to vote predictably based on the demands of single-issue groups and lobbies.

Plebiscitary Democracy

One proposal that surfaced during the Perot candidacy was reminiscent of calls issued as early as the late 1970s for plebiscitary initiatives in the name of promoting democratic citizenship, although, in fact, it undermines the democracy it purports to bolster. I refer to schemes for instant plebiscites via interactive television or telepolling celebrated by their proponents as a technologically more perfect democracy. But plebiscitary majoritarianism is quite different from a democratic polity sustained by debate and judgment. Plebiscites have often sought to shore up antidemocratic regimes — Peronism in Argentina and Pinochet in Chile come to mind. In a plebiscitary system, the views of the majority by definition swamp minority or unpopular views.

Plebiscitarianism is compatible with authoritarian politics carried out under the guise of, or with the connivance of, the ritualistic registering of majority opinion. There is no need for debate with one's fellow citizens on substantive questions. All that is required is a calibration of opinion that, once voiced, solidifies into affirmation or negation of simplistically presented alternatives. Citizens and legislators alike are stripped of the possibility and duty of deliberation and choice. Being asked to proffer an opinion and to register it instantly seems democratic. But he or she expressing an opinion is reduced to a private person by contrast to the public citizen liberal democracy presumes and requires. Tying the 25 percent decline in associational memberships over the past quarter-century to a number of phenomena, Robert Putnam notes that the "most obvious and probably the most powerful instrument of this revolution is television" (Putnam, 25). What televoting would do is to fully legitimate our loss of sociality by making it possible for us to register a political opinion or "taste" as private persons, enclosed within ourselves, rather than as public citizens. To see button-pressing as a meaningful act on a par with lobbying, meeting neighbors, serving on the local school board, working for a candidate, or helping to forge a coalition to promote a particular program or policy parallels a crude version of so-called preference theory in economics.

This theory holds that in a free-market society, the sum total of individual consumer choices results in the greatest benefit to society as a whole even as these choices meet individual "needs." The assumption is that each of us is a "preference maximizer." Aside from being a simplistic account of human motivation, it denies the possibility of social goods — there are only aggregates of private goods. Measuring our opinions through "electronic town halls" is a variant on this crude but common notion. The cure it promises is more of precisely what ails us. Under the banner of more perfected democratic choice, we shall erode even further those elements of deliberation, reason, judgment, and shared goodwill that alone make genuine choice, hence democracy, possible. We would complete the ongoing process of turning our representatives into factotums, mouthpieces expressing our electronically generated "will."

The Future of Our Democracy

The tale here told traces the unraveling of the institutions of civil society, hence the dramatic upsurge in all forms of social mistrust and generalized fearfulness and cynicism, to the current crisis of governing I have called a spiral of delegitimation. Recent studies show that Americans of all races "cite the same social problems: crime, poor education, imperiled sanctity of home and family."[5] Indeed, if anything, black Americans are more insistent that their society faces a crisis in values, beginning with the family. But there is less agreement on why things have gone wrong and what can be done to put them right. "More economic opportunity" is cited, vaguely but persistently, as a goal for blacks, who also express almost no confidence in American legal institutions or politics, yet want "government" to create jobs and opportunities. Whites see a smaller role for government but not surprisingly, given recent developments, neither whites nor blacks express confidence in the institutions of liberal democratic society. Both groups, in other words, seem ripe for Perot-type "direct democracy" efforts and both seem equally susceptible to the distortion of democratic debate in the hands of media scandalmongers and unscrupulous demagogues. This is a situation begging for a true democratic debate and courageous leadership and wise legislation.

The sociologist Robert Bellah reports that Americans today brighten to tales of community, especially if the talk is soothing and doesn't appear to demand very much from them. Yet when the discussion turns to the need to sustain and to support authoritative civic institutions, attention withers and a certain sourness arises. This bodes ill for liberal democratic society, a political regime that requires robust yet resilient institutions that embody and reflect, yet mediate and shape, the urgencies or democratic passions and interests. As our mediating institutions, from the PTA to political parties, disappear or are stripped of legitimacy, a political wilderness spreads. People roam the prairie fixing on objects or policies or persons to excoriate or to celebrate, at least for a time until some other enthusiasm or scandal sweeps over them. If we have lost the sturdiness and patience necessary to sustain civil society over the long haul, liberal democracy itself — as a system, a social world, and a culture — is in trouble.

Notes

1. See, for example, Robert D. Putnam, "Bowling Alone: Democracy in America at the End of the Twentieth Century," which summarizes the empirical data on the sharp and insistent plummeting of civic engagement in the United States. (Unpublished paper, Department of Government, Harvard University, August 1994). Cited with permission.

2. See, for example, Sylvia Ann Hewlett, *When the Bough Breaks: The Cost of Neglecting Our Children* (New York: Basic Books, 1991); and Jean Bethke Elshtain, "Family Matters," *Christian Century*, July 14-21, 1993, 710-711.

3. "U.S. Voters Focus on Selves, Poll Says," *New York Times*, September 21, 1994, A-21.

4. "The People, The Press and Politics: The New Political Landscape," *Times-Mirror* survey, September 21, 1994.

5. Gerald F. Seib and Joe Davidson, "Whites, Blacks Agree on Problems; the Issue is How to Solve Them," *Wall Street Journal*, September 29, 1994, A-1, A-6.

Diversity and Difference

Chapter 6

Indians and Mexican Americans

Richard Rodriguez

Indians

Igrew up in Sacramento thinking of Indians as people who had disappeared. I was a Mexican in California; I would no more have thought of myself as an Aztec in California than you might imagine yourself a Viking or a Bantu. Mrs. Ferrucci up the block used to call my family "Spanish." We know she intended to ennoble us by that designation. We also knew she was ignorant.

I was ignorant.

In America the Indian is relegated to the obligatory first chapter — the "Once Great Nation" chapter — after which the Indian is cleared away as easily as brush, using a very sharp rhetorical tool called an "alas." Thereafter, the Indian reappears only as a stunned remnant — Ishi, or the hundred-year-old hag blowing out her birthday candle at a rest home in Tucson; or the teenager drunk on his ass in Plaza Park.

Here they come down Broadway in the Fourth of July parades of my childhood — middle-aged men wearing glasses, beating their tom-toms; Hey-ya-ya; Hey-ya-ya. They wore Bermuda shorts under their loincloths. High-school kids could never refrain from the answering Woo-woo-woo, stopping their mouths with the palms of their hands.

In the 1960s, Indians began to name themselves Native Americans, recalling themselves to life. That self-designation underestimated the ruthless idea Puritans had superimposed upon the landscape. America is an idea to which natives are inimical. The Indian represented permanence and continuity to Americans who were determined to call this country new. Indians must be ghosts.

I collected conflicting evidence concerning Mexico, it's true, but I never felt myself the remnant of anything. Mexican magazines arrived in our mailbox from Mexico City; showed pedestrians strolling wide ocher boulevards beneath trees with lime-green leaves. My past was at least this coherent:

Mexico was a real place with plenty of people walking around in it. My parents had come from somewhere that went on without them.

When I was a graduate student at Berkeley, teaching remedial English, there were a few American Indians in my classroom. They were unlike any other "minority students" in the classes I taught. The Indians drifted in and out. When I summoned them to my office, they came and sat while I did all the talking.

I remember one tall man particularly, a near-somnambulist, beautiful in an off-putting way, but interesting, too, because I never saw him without the current issue of *The New York Review of Books* under his arm, which I took as an advertisement of ambition. He eschewed my class for weeks at a time. Then one morning I saw him in a café on Telegraph Avenue, across from Cody's. I did not fancy myself Sidney Poitier, but I was interested in this moody brave's lack of interest in me, for one, and then *The New York Review*.

Do you mind if I sit here?

Nothing.

Blah, Blah, Blah . . . N.Y.R.B.? — entirely on my part — until, when I got up to leave:

You're not Indian, you're Mexican, he said. You wouldn't understand.

He meant I was cut. Diluted.

Understand what?

He meant I was not an Indian in America. He meant he was an enemy of the history that had otherwise created me. And he was right, I didn't understand. I took his diffidence for chauvinism. I read his chauvinism as arrogance. He didn't see the Indian in my face? I saw his face — his refusal to consort with the living — as the face of a dead man.

As the landscape goes, so goes the Indian? In the public-service TV commercial, the Indian sheds a tear at the sight of an America polluted beyond his recognition. Indian memory has become the measure against which America gauges corrupting history when it suits us. Gitchigoomeism — the habit of placing the Indian outside history — is a white sentimentality that relegates the Indian to death.

An obituary from *The New York Times* (September 1989 — dateline Alaska): An oil freighter has spilled its load along the Alaskan coast. There is a billion-dollar cleanup, bringing jobs and dollars to Indian villages.

The modern world has been closing in on English Bay . . . with glacial slowness. The oil spill and the resulting sea of money have accelerated the process, so that English Bay now seems caught on the cusp of history.

The omniscient reporter from *The New York Times* takes it upon himself to regret history on behalf of the Indians.

Instead of hanging salmon to dry this month, as Aleut natives have done for centuries . . . John Kvasnikoff was putting up a three thousand dollar television satellite dish on the bluff next to his home above the sea.

The reporter from *The New York Times* knows the price modernity will exact from an Indian who wants to plug himself in. Mind you, the reporter is confident of his own role in history, his freedom to lug a word processor to some remote Alaskan village. About the reporter's journey, *The New York Times* is not censorious. But let the Indian drop one bead from custom, or let his son straddle a snowmobile — as he does in the photo accompanying the article — and *The New York Times* cries Boo-hoo-hoo yah-yah-yah.

Thus does the Indian become the mascot of an international ecology movement. The industrial countries of the world romanticize the Indian who no longer exists, ignoring the Indian who does — the Indian who is poised to chop down his rain forest, for example. Or the Indian who reads *The New York Times*.

Once more in San Francisco: I flattered myself that the woman staring at me all evening "knew my work," I considered myself an active agent, in other words. But, after several passes around the buffet, the woman cornered me to say she recognized me as an "ancient soul."

Do I lure or am I just minding my own business?

Is it the nature of Indians — not verifiable in nature, of course, but in the European description of Indians — that we wait around to be "discovered"?

Europe discovers. India beckons. Isn't that so? India sits atop her lily pad through centuries, lost in contemplation of the horizon. And, from time to time, India is discovered.

In the fifteenth century, sailing Spaniards were acting according to scientific conjecture as to the nature and as to the shape of the world. Most thinking men in Europe at the time of Columbus believed the world to be round. The voyage of Columbus was the test of a theory believed to be true. Brave, yes, but pedantic therefore.

The Indian is forever implicated in the roundness of the world. America was the false India, the mistaken India, and yet veritable India, for all that — India — the clasp, the coupling mystery at the end of quest.

This is as true today as of yore. Where do the Beatles go when the world is too much with them? Where does Jerry Brown seek the fat farm of his soul? India, man, India!

India waits.

India has all the answers beneath her passive face or behind her veil or between her legs. The European has only questions, questions that are assertions turned inside out, questions that can only be answered by sailing toward the abysmal horizon.

The lusty Europeans wanted the shortest answers. They knew what they wanted. They wanted spices, pagodas, gold.

Had the world been flat, had the European sought the unknown, then the European would have been as great a victor over history as he has portrayed himself to be. The European would have outdistanced history — even theology — if he could have arrived at the shore of some prelapsarian state. If the world had been flat, then the European could have traveled outward toward innocence.

But the world was round. The entrance into the Indies was a reunion of peoples. The Indian awaited the long-separated European, the inevitable European, as the approaching horizon.

Though perhaps, too, there was some demiurge felt by the human race of the fifteenth century to heal itself, to make itself whole? Certainly, in retrospect, there was some inevitability to the Catholic venture. If the world was round, continuous, then so, too, were peoples?

According to the European version — the stag version — of the pageant of the New World, the Indian must play a passive role. Europe has been accustomed to play the swaggart in history — Europe striding through the Americas, overturning temples, spilling language, spilling seed, spilling blood.

And wasn't the Indian the female, the passive, the waiting aspect to the theorem — lewd and promiscuous in her embrace as she is indolent betimes?

Charles Macomb Flandrau, a native of St. Paul, Minnesota, wrote a book called *Viva Mexico!* in 1908, wherein he described the Mexican Indian as "incorrigibly plump." One never ceases to marvel at the superhuman strength existing beneath the pretty and effeminate modeling of their arms and legs and backs. . . . "The legs of an American 'strong man' look usually like an anatomical chart, but the legs of the most powerful Totonac Indian — and the power of many of them is beyond belief — would serve admirably as one of those idealized extremities on which women's hosiery is displayed in shop windows."

In Western Civilization histories, the little honeymoon joke Europe tells on itself is of mistaking America for the extremities of India. But India was perhaps not so much a misnomer as was "discoverer" or "conquistador."

Earliest snapshots of Indians brought back to Europe were of naked little woodcuts, arms akimbo, resembling Erasmus, or of grandees in capes and feathered tiaras, courtiers of an Egyptified palace of nature. In European museums, she is idle, recumbent at the base of a silver pineapple tree or the pedestal of the Dresden urn or the Sèvres tureen — the use of European adventure, at once wanderlust and bounty.

Many tribes of Indians were prescient enough, preserved memory enough, or were lonesome enough to predict the coming of a pale stranger from across the sea, a messianic twin of completing memory or skill.

None of this could the watery Europeans have known as they marveled at the sight of approaching land. Filled with the arrogance of discovery, the Europeans were not predisposed to imagine that they were being watched, awaited.

That friend of mine at Oxford loses patience whenever I describe my face as mestizo. Look at my face. What do you see?

An Indian, he says.

Mestizo, I correct.

Mestizo, mestizo, he says.

Listen, he says. I went back to my mother's village in Mexico last summer and there was nothing mestizo about it. Dust, dogs, and Indians. People there don't even speak Spanish.

So, I ask my friend at Oxford what it means to him to be an Indian.

He hesitates. My friend has recently been taken up as amusing by a bunch of rich Pakistanis in London. But, facing me, he is vexed and in earnest.

He describes a lonely search among his family for evidence of Indian-ness. He thinks he has found it in his mother; watching his mother in her garden.

Does she plant corn by the light of the moon?

She seems to have some relationship with the earth, he says quietly.

So there it is. The mystical tie to nature. How else to think of the Indian except in terms of some druidical green thumb? No one says of an English matron in her rose garden that she is behaving like a Celt. Because the Indian has no history — that is, because history books are the province of the descendants of Europeans — the Indian seems only to belong to the party of the first part, the first chapter. So that is where the son expects to find his mother, Daughter of the Moon.

Let's talk about something else. Let's talk about London. The last time I was in London, I was walking toward an early evening at the Queen's Theater when I passed that Christopher Wren church near Fortnum & Mason. The church was lit; I decided to stop, to savor the spectacle of what I expected would be a few Pymish men and women rolled into balls of fur at Evensong. Imagine my surprise that the congregation was young — dressed in army fatigues and Laura Ashley. Within the chancel, cross-legged on a dais, was a South American shaman.

Now, who is the truer Indian in this picture? Me . . . me on my way to the Queen's Theater? Or that guy on the altar with a Ph.D. in death?

Mexican Americans

In 1959, Octavio Paz, Mexico's sultan son, her clever one — philosopher, poet, statesman — published *The Labyrinth of Solitude*, his reflections on Mexico. Within his labyrinth, Paz places as well the Mexican American. He writes of the *pachuco*, the teenage gang member and, by implication, of the Mexican American: "The *pachuco* does not want to become a Mexican again; at the same time he does not want to blend into the life of North America. His whole being is sheer negative impulse, a tangle of contradictions, an enigma."

This was Mother Mexico talking, her good son; this was Mexico's metropolitan version of Mexican Americans. Mexico had lost language, lost gods, lost ground. Mexico recognized historical confusion in us. We were Mexico's Mexicans.

In his glass apartment overlooking the Polanco district of Mexico City, the journalist says he does not mind in the least that I call myself an American. "But when I hear Mexicans in the United States talk about George Washington as the father of their country," he exhales a florid ellipsis of cigarette smoke.

America does not lend itself to sexual metaphor as easily as Mexico does. George Washington is the father of the country, we say. We speak of Founding Fathers. The legend ascribed to the Statue of Liberty is childlessness.

America is an immigrant country. Motherhood — parenthood — is less our point than adoption. If I had to assign gender to America, I would notice the consensus of the rest of the world. When America is burned in effigy, a male is burned. Americans themselves speak of Uncle Sam. Uncle Sam is the personification of conscription.

During World War II, hundreds of thousands of Mexican Americans were drafted to fight in Europe and in Asia. And they went submitting themselves to a commonweal. Not a very Mexican thing to do, for Mexico had taught us always that we lived apart from history in the realm of *tú*.

It was Uncle Sam who shaved the sideburns from that generation of Mexican Americans. Like the Goddess of Liberty, Uncle Sam has no children of his own. In a way, Sam represents necessary evil to the American imagination. He steals children to make men of them, mocks all reticence, all modesty, all memory. Uncle Sam is a hectoring Yankee, a skinflint uncle, gaunt, uncouth, unloved. He is the American Savonarola — hater of moonshine, destroyer of stills, burner of cocaine. Free enterprise is curiously an evasion of Uncle Sam, as is sentimentality. Sam has no patience with mamas' boys. That includes Mama Mexico, ma'am.

You betray Uncle Sam by favoring private over public life, by seeking to exempt yourself: by cheating on your income taxes, by avoiding jury duty, by trying to keep your boy on the farm. These are legal offenses.

Betrayal of Mother Mexico, on the other hand, is a sin against the natural law, a failure of memory.

When the war was over, Mexican Americans returned home to a GI Bill and with the expectation of an improved future. By the 1950s, Mexican Americans throughout the Southwest were busy becoming middle class. I would see them around Sacramento: a Mexican-American dentist; a shoe salesman at Weinstock's; the couple that ran the tiny Mexican food store that became, before I graduated from high school, a block-long electrified MEXICATESSEN. These were not "role models," exactly; they were people like my parents, making their way in America.

When I was in grammar school, they used to hit us for speaking Spanish.
THEY.

Mexican Americans forfeit the public experience of America because we fear it. And for decades in the American Southwest, public life was withheld from us. America lay north of *usted*, beyond even formal direct address. America was the realm of *los norteamericanos* — They. We didn't have an adequate name for you. In private, you were the gringo. The ethnic albino. The goyim.

The ghost. You were not us. In public we also said "Anglo" — an arcane usage of the nineteenth century — you-who-speak-English. If we withdrew from directly addressing you, you became *ellos* — They — as in: They kept us on the other side of town. They owned the land. They owned the banks. They ran the towns — they and their wives in their summer-print dresses. They kept wages low. They made us sit upstairs in the movie houses. Or downstairs.

Thus spoken memory becomes a kind of shorthand for some older, other outrage, the nineteenth-century affront. The land stolen. The Mexican scorned on land he had named. Spic. Greaser. Spanish, the great metropolitan language, reduced to a foreign tongue, a language of the outskirts, the language of the gibbering poor, thus gibberish; English, the triumphal, crushing metaphor.

I know Mexican Americans who have lived in this country for forty or fifty years and have never applied for citizenship or gathered more than a Montgomery Ward sense of English. Their refusal, lodged between *How much and Okay*, is not a linguistic dilemma primarily.

On the other hand, when we call ourselves Mexican Americans, Mexico is on the phone, long-distance: *So typical of the gringo's arrogance to appropriate the name of a hemisphere to himself— yes? But why should you repeat the folly?*

Mexico always can find a myth to account for us: Mexicans who go north are like the Chichimeca — a barbarous tribe antithetical to Mexico. But in the United States, Mexican Americans did not exist in the national imagination until the 1960s — years when the black civil rights movement prompted Americans to acknowledge "invisible minorities" in their midst. Then it was determined statistically that Mexican Americans constituted a disadvantaged society, living in worse conditions than most other Americans, having less education, facing bleaker sidewalks or Safeways.

Bueno. (Again Mother Mexico is on the phone.) *What kind of word is that— "minority"? Was the Mexican American—* she fries the term on the skillet of her tongue *— was the Mexican American content to say that his association with Mexico left him culturally disadvantaged?*

The sixties were years of romance for the American middle class. Americans competed with one another to play the role of society's victim. It was an age of T-shirts.

In those years, the national habit of Americans was to seek from the comparison with blacks a kind of analogy. Mexican-American political activists, especially student activists, insisted on a rough similarity between the two societies — black, Chicano — ignoring any complex factor of history or race that might disqualify the equation.

Black Americans had suffered relentless segregation and mistreatment, but blacks had been implicated in the public life of this country from the beginning. Oceans separated the black slave from any possibility of rescue or restoration. From the symbiosis of oppressor and the oppressed, blacks took a hard realism. They acquired the language of the white man, though they inflected it with refusal. And because racism fell upon all blacks, regardless of class, a bond developed between the poor and the bourgeoisie, thence the possibility of a leadership class able to speak for the entire group.

Mexican Americans of the generation of the sixties had no myth of themselves as Americans. So that when Mexican Americans won national notoriety, we could only refer the public gaze to the past. We are people of the land, we told ourselves. Middle-class college students took to wearing farmer-in-the-dell overalls and they took, as well, a rural slang to name themselves: Chicanos.

Chicanismo blended nostalgia with grievance to reinvent the mythic northern kingdom of Atzlán as corresponding to the Southwestern American desert. Just as Mexico would only celebrate her Indian half, Chicanos determined to portray themselves as Indians in America, as indigenous people, thus casting the United States in the role of Spain.

Chicanos used the language of colonial Spain to declare to America that they would never give up their culture. And they said, in Spanish, that Spaniards had been oppressors of their people.

Left to ourselves in a Protestant land, Mexican Americans shored up our grievances, making of them altars to the past. *May my tongue cleave to my palate if I should forget thee. (Tú.)*

Ah, Mother, can you not realize how Mexican we have become?

But she hates us, she hates us.

Chicanismo offended Mexico. It was one thing for Mexico to play the victim among her children, but Mexico did not like it that Chicanos were playing the same role for the gringos.

By claiming too many exemptions, Chicanos also offended Americans. Chicanos seemed to violate a civic agreement that generations of other immigrants had honored: *My* grandparents had to learn English. . . .

Chicanos wanted more and less than they actually said. On the one hand, Chicanos were intent upon bringing America (as a way of bringing history) to some Act of Contrition. On the other hand, Chicanos sought pride, a restoration of face in America. And America might provide the symbolic solution to a Mexican dilemma: if one could learn public English while yet retaining family Spanish, *usted* might be reunited with *tú*, the future might be reconciled with the past.

Mexicans are a people of sacraments and symbols. I think few Chicanos ever expected Spanish to become a public language coequal with English. But by demanding Spanish in the two most symbolic places of American citizenship — the classroom and the voting booth — Chicanos were consoling themselves that they need not give up the past to participate in the American city. They were not less American for speaking Spanish; they were not less Mexican for succeeding in America.

America got bored with such altars — too Catholic for the likes of America. Protestant America is a literal culture.

SAY WHAT YOU WANT.

What was granted was a bureaucratic bilingualism — classrooms and voting booths — pragmatic concessions to a spiritual grievance.

I end up arguing about bilingualism with other Mexican Americans, middle-class like myself. As I am my father's son, I am skeptical, like Mexico; I play the heavy, which is to say I play America. We argue and argue, but not about pedagogy. We argue about desire's reach; we exchange a few platitudes (being richer for having two languages; being able to go home again). In the end, the argument reduces to somebody's childhood memory.

When I was in school, they used to hit us for speaking Spanish.

My father says the trouble with the bilingual voting ballot is that one ends up voting for the translator.

Chapter 7

A Hispanic Writer Takes a Look at the United States

Elena Castedo

The United States is a showcase for everything that human beings can be or do when individuality, respect for human rights, and freedom are idolized. It is a laboratory, a circus, a repository of universal folklore, a research center, a zoo, a repair shop, a freak show, a training institution, an amusement park, and a perpetual premiere of the future. Everyone speaks, dresses, and grows fat as they darn well please. A descendant of four generations of Harvard graduates gets replaced by the son or daughter of an illiterate Asian immigrant. The poor drive their cars to pick up their welfare checks sporting Olympic running shoes.

Everything is done to its limit; everything is "done." If Europe was the maquette for America, then the United States is the building — with completely unexpected readjustments and details. If Europe took its string quartet to America, the United States transformed it into an orchestra. English humor turned into loud laughter. Even when smallness becomes fashionable, it is done on a grand scale.

Everybody sees in the United States whatever he or she wants to see: place your eyes here, search there, weigh here, consider there; you will witness, find, and judge what you wish. As H.L. Mencken affirmed, whatever you might say about the United States is true. And the opposite is also true. Something said today may be the exact opposite tomorrow. Therefore, any valid opinion about the United States must be formulated in a historical perspective, to extract from that fragmented and changing whirlwind the Prometheus within.

The problem is that this Prometheus goes by the name of paradox. Of all the nations of the world, it is in the United States where the revolution — an intrinsic part of the national character — has kept its most vital momentum,

Translated by Roberto Tejada with the author. A section of this article appeared as "U.S.A.: America Seen by Its Writers," in *Diario 16*, Madrid, June 31, 1994; and as "To Be Hispanic and Write in English," in *Diario 16*, Madrid, October 10, 1992.

remaining as strong as when it was born. Although the principles established
by the founding fathers tie the country to the past, those very principles are an
enticement to forsake the past. Power is granted by vote, but backs are promptly
turned on the elected leaders, leaving public power in the hands of the mass
media and private power in the small hands of children. A secular country that
fears official religion like the plague, where deodorants are worshipped like
gods, the United States watches impotently as pseudo-Buddhist gurus and
evangelist ministers become multimillionaires recruiting bored women and
youngsters and petitioning money on television from the elderly.

On the one hand, the United States is the most international of all
countries, a perpetual world's fair on display in the streets, offices, institutions, factories, businesses, temples, books, and the world of entertainment.
All languages are spoken, all foods are served, all traditional garbs are worn,
all religions are practiced. Thousands of newspapers are read in a multitude
of languages. In my house, we receive several newspapers and magazines
in Spanish, as well as one in Catalan, all published in the United States. Our
television at home receives broadcasts in Spanish, French, Italian, Farsi,
Arabic, Korean, Japanese, Creole, and other languages that are a total mystery
to me. According to the latest statistics, at least one foreign language is
spoken in 46 percent of all urban households, Spanish at the forefront.

On the other hand, this multinationality coexists with an entrenched
provincialism. As if native countries disappeared the moment emigrants left
them, international coverage in the press concentrates only on the spectacular, the gruesome, and the tragic. As if the United States were not just the navel
of the world but the world itself, the majority of its citizens — whether new
or from long ago — think that whatever happens in the country could happen
only in America. In the only nation where there are no "foreigners," as soon
as immigrants arrive (more than a million illegally per year alone), they learn
to complain indignantly about not living as well as they deserve, having
instantly forgotten the hunger and the dictatorships that forced them to leave
their native lands.

The United States is proud of its struggle to increase respect for personal
dignity, of its inventions to improve the living standards of the human race,
of its contributions to ideas and art. But at the same time, it shows no mercy
when punishing itself, assuming responsibility for all the social ills common
to all of humanity, as if the United States were the only place in which these
flaws could flourish. While citizens of the United States privately send
millions to other nations for charitable or educational purposes, its political
leaders periodically undertake quixotic and demented endeavors aimed at
exporting U.S. ideology, if not by reason, then by force. In this, the United
States resembles a Saint Bernard who makes a life-saving rescue and then
wags it tail with such enthusiasm that it knocks someone down the mountain.

The United States' noble motto is the "pursuit of happiness," but citizens
work seven days a week. Most Latin Americans who visit relatives living in
the United States are surprised. Some, because they find them in crowded,
dingy neighborhoods without a single hot tub from which to contemplate a
panoramic view of Los Angeles, as seen in Hollywood movies. On the

contrary, their relatives work day and night "in pursuit" of that hot tub. Other visitors are surprised to find their relatives in the United States living in "luxury" houses with lush gardens and vast green lawns. It is hard for them to imagine that these home owners are immigrants, bureaucrats, teachers, plumbers, soldiers, chefs, nurses, or small businessmen who perhaps invent household items or import rugs. They are not rich; nor are they executives, physicians, lawyers, or bankers. So, how can they afford a gardener, a painter, a carpenter, etc., for surely, "a house that big needs constant upkeep." We do it all ourselves, they hear, as they are escorted to an arsenal of work tools and building supplies. "But, when do you have time for all this?" On weekends, at night, and during the summer when we can take a couple of weeks off. "But, then, when do you ever rest or take a vacation?" We don't.

Until a few years ago, the United States had to create a sense of national identity by encouraging a rapid assimilation of cultures. Despite the civil rights achievements during the 1950s and 1960s, the process of assimilation for Afro-Americans has been gradual and complex, creating an unsettling polarization. (The sector of Native Americans is visible but significantly smaller.) In the midst of this tense and troubled situation, Hispanics became for the first time visible. Many believe that after Mexico, Spain, and either Argentina or Colombia, the United States ranks fourth in Hispanic population — which is estimated at more than twenty-three million, with probably several more uncounted millions. Hispanics are neither black nor white, which in some ways may have helped to dilute the predominant racial polarity. Asian Americans remain far behind in demographic and political power, though they are rapidly becoming an important economic and professional force. Perhaps in the 1980s, this new Hispanic presence helped to launch the fashionable social concept of "ethnicity." For the first time, "diversity," not assimilation, is celebrated.

Nevertheless, ethnicity and language are sent their separate ways. While multilingualism exists in private, the use of languages other than English in public elicits discomfort at best, if not blatant hostility, from English speakers. To be Hispanic in the United States has least to do with speaking Spanish. It is not even related to the possession of a sizable Hispanic cultural baggage. It means having ancestors who came to the United States from any of the countries in which the majority speaks Castilian. An Aymará Indian who does not speak Spanish and never had an ancestor who did is a Hispanic. In the United States, the term "ethnic" does not refer, as it does in other languages, to race but rather to a group that preserves characteristics of a social group that is not the dominant one. Hispanics come from all kinds of backgrounds but particularly from the blend of indigenous, Spanish, and black cultures. Although there are publishing houses and magazines, whether they be commercial, literary, or university publications, that print works by Hispanic writers in both English and Spanish (in addition to scores of other organizations concerned with Hispanics), there are also millions of Hispanics in the United States who barely know a word of Spanish and who have never heard of Cervantes, unless, oh, you mean that neighbor who worked in the meat section of the local supermarket?

"Ethnicity" may be fashionable in the 1990s, but the United States is still a monolingual country. If you are "American," you speak English. We can accept tacos, pizza, chow mein, sushi, and a foreign word here and there, but for heaven's sake, no multilingualism. How do we know that a language other than English may not be a Greek horse that will unleash a Trojan blood bath? This fear has found its most fanatic outlet in the "English only" movement, whose obvious aim is to declare illegal the official use of Spanish in the United States. How long "ethnicity," "diversity," and "multiculturalism" will remain fashionable and how long before, if ever, a more tolerant multilingualism will emerge are questions that the twenty-first century will answer.

Neither saint nor whore, the United States is like the village woman who defies convention, disdained but secretly desired by men, criticized and hated but inwardly admired by women. For decades — aside from matters of foreign policy that deserve criticism — one of the favorite pastimes among bourgeois intellectuals in Latin America has been to throw stones at the United States. Favored targets of scorn and sneers are its "love affair" with the automobile, its gadgets, its dehumanizing supermarkets, its racism, its drug addicts. In the second part of the twentieth century, we have witnessed two inescapable facts: one, that all the social flaws common in the United States have become common throughout the world. (In Latin America, they are worse in underprivileged neighborhoods, which the stone throwers observe with binoculars from a safe distance.) And two, that in all countries, the bourgeoisie and all those who so aspire have developed even more passionate love affairs with the automobile, domestic gadgets, and supermarkets. Today Latin Americans are irritated by the U.S. "obsession" against smoking; they are appalled by the riots that erupt in neighborhoods where ethnic minorities live at the poverty level; they are horrified by juvenile crimes. It would be wiser if all of us observed critically our own surroundings.

We all live in glass houses, where we are vulnerable even to members of our own families. Instead of pretending that the rest of the world appears and disappears according to the interests of the moment — as the United States often does — and instead of wasting time throwing useless stones at others — the way Latin America often does — we would all benefit by observing and learning not only to imitate the most useful aspects of each culture, but to discard notions that are seemingly useful but in the long run create more problems than they solve. We need to reinforce the roofs above our heads, because whenever a taste for individuality, human rights and freedom develops, catapults get poised at the ready.

Chapter 8

In the Shadow of Prefabricated Gods

Todd Gitlin

Our secular twentieth century has known two great universalizing passions: "universalizing" in their assertion that humanity has a common nature and a common destiny, "passions" in the sense of world views affirmed with a depth of conviction that led millions of people to sacrifice their lives in their names.

On the one hand was Marxism, affirming a commonality rooted in membership in a steadily growing working class, the class to end all classes, whose hypothetical all-unifying existence, however, lay in the future, indefinitely postponed, on the far side of the class struggle to end all class struggles. Whatever the facts, this was an ingenious idea in its structure. It began by acknowledging enormous differences in circumstances — a few owned the means of production and wealth, while the vast majority worked for wages, usually in dreadful conditions. From this observation, Marxist theory leaped to an apocalyptic claim about the common destiny of all workers: namely, that they would become ever more numerous, ever more miserable, ever more exploited, and ever more bonded with each other, so that, eventually, they could reach out and pluck from the owners the productive property that would guarantee a decent and fulfilling life for all. The genius of the idea lay in the claim that the diversity of the population was being processed automatically into a sort of universality.

Very much on the other hand was the principle of the extension of individual rights, as enshrined in the American Declaration of Independence ("all men are endowed by their Creator with inalienable rights,...among these...life, liberty, and the pursuit of happiness") and in the French Declaration of the Rights of Man and of Citizen. As with Marxism, this world view contained an irony: The rights of the individual would be guaranteed by a vast and abstract entity, the nation-state. The genius of the American idea was the presumption that concentrations of power were unjust because they interfered with the capacity of society — individual property holders and their associations, for the most part — for self-regulation. The French idea placed more stock in reason imposed from above by the state. But the two revolutions had in common a presumption that ordinary people were entitled to make history and a faith in what the people could do if left to their own devices.

According to these Enlightenment principles, anyone from anywhere could affiliate. In this sense, both world views were affirmations of freedom. Both fused the modern Western faith in the active molding of history with a conviction that progress was already unfolding. Born in rebellion, both established themselves as major organizing forces shaping human society in the twentieth century. Today, both are damaged — one fatally, the other perhaps not. The problem much of the world wrestles with is how to imagine a common world without their vigor. An Enlightenment of inclusion seems beyond us.

Obviously, liberalism and Marxism have affirmed quite different premises, produced decidedly different results, and enjoy quite different states of health. Marxism today is generally understood to be bankrupt, although radical movements continue to write bad checks on an overdrawn account. Nevertheless, the two share a common taproot in the Enlightenment: a faith in the capacity of reason to knit together humanity. In this sense, the convulsive transformations of 1989-1990 might signal not simply the end of three-quarters of a century of a dreadful historical turn but also the resumption of an uncompleted Enlightenment. Or it might, as religious fundamentalists think, signal the repudiation of the Enlightenment altogether. Certainly, at this moment, fundamentalists of various stripes are pursuing their own universalist crusades against the forces of secularism.

One might expect that defenders of individual rights would be basking today in the bright sunlight of ideological victory. The adversary was not only routed, it fled the battlefield, leaving the ruins of Stalinism surrounded by a surreal marketplace as a perverse memorial to the grim absurdity of statist socialism. One might think that, once the rubble of history had been swept away, we could manage without all the false universalisms, each with its grotesque idea of what human beings may be compelled to do. One might hope that now we could get back to a modest reason, so that reformers would no longer compete to see into which interesting shapes human nature can be twisted.

Yet the implosion of Marxism-Leninism has not erased extravagant intentions from the world. Instead, the triumphant individualism of rights gets collapsed commonly into a single right: the right of capital to increase. That right seems triumphant. The conquest of one wing of the Enlightenment by the other is incontestable. The market is everywhere trumpeted as the sole source of economic growth and the undisputed marker of social health. One hears everywhere, in South as in North America, in much of Asia and in the former Soviet Union as in present-day Europe, that social problems can be reduced simply by removing impediments to the flow of capital.

Capitalism's Destructive Force

Yet a balance sheet is no basis for a moral community. Capital is revolutionary, imposing ideas on the material world, emptying out the countryside, churning up huge cities, commanding the air and the sea. Like all revolutions, it disturbs the balance of life. Capital has no conscience. The economic system of capitalism is compatible with a very wide range of social and political arrangements: fascism, liberalism, gangsterism, theocracy, social democracy.

Moreover, the triumph of capitalism does not by itself make for the satisfactions that add up to the stability of a social order. Normally, it is true, it does produce middle classes, the historical bulwarks of democracy. But in the economically advanced world, what the sociologist Ben Agger calls "fast capitalism" has contrary effects as well. As we approach the close of the century with only one economic system in place, capital is increasingly movable, exercising unprecedented and virtually unimpeded mobility from high-wage to lower-wage regions, from rich countries to poor, from labor-intensive production to capital-intensive. Capital creates wealth and jobs in some regions and converts other regions to fields of beggars. In the affluent West, it hollows out middle classes and weakens state systems of social security. As short-sighted elites enrich themselves, the populations divide: above, a narrow band of managers and professionals who live by their wits and their work; below, the growing numbers of the poor; between, the middle sectors working for stagnating wages, worrying about criminals and immigrants, taking refuge behind "security systems" within "gated communities."

Such controls as Western societies succeeded in imposing on capital's freedom of movement during the past century are eroding. Growth is uneven; debt is mountainous; inequality is immense; fear is endemic. The state, as a result, is compelled to do more, but deprived of the means to do so. Observing the state's incapacity, people doubt democratic institutions. Largely for this reason, social democracy is in disarray and recoils throughout the industrial world. Communities are defenseless against capital's propensity to pick up and go where the action is bigger, better, quicker. In the United States, trade unions have dwindled to the point that only one American worker in nine belongs to a union today. Management-union relations have regressed to their condition of 70 years ago. The experience of class solidarity is at its lowest ebb in three-quarters of a century. Even many workers see unions as bureaucracies that pursue "special interests."

In the United States, and in varying degrees throughout the industrialized world, the result of these tendencies is a loss of faith in democratic institutions. When people think of the *res publica*, the public sector, they tend to think of unsafe streets and bad schools. It is primarily the private sector that is associated with efficiency — Federal Express and UPS as opposed to the U.S. Postal Service. The public buses are infrequent and overloaded, while limousines glide by. The people waiting in line blame the state, from which they wish to withdraw their subsidies.

Capital, on the other hand, shows results. Capital is a dynamo: It innovates. It is the device with which some individuals succeed in writing their scripts in the world, and for each who succeeds, many others make the attempt or hope to do so. Capital carries a sense of adventure, of free undertaking — thus the word "enterprise," literally an undertaking. But the spirit of enterprise tends to be captured within one powerful force-field: the ambitions of individuals. Despite the numbers of those who profess religious belief, the ambition to make money is not matched by the ambition to do good on a scale larger than the individual family. Capitalism remains, as Joseph Schumpeter said, a system of creative destruction — destructive of social bonds, faiths, communities, traditions.

A Shrill Individualism

As an ideal, however, buccaneer individualism rides high. In the United States, the Reagan decade enshrined ideals of entrepreneurship and privatization and heightened Americans' traditional suspicion of the state. Although excesses of personal thievery have been deplored and at times punished, the ideal of the self-sufficient, free-standing individual swashbuckling his way through the world continues to reign. This ideal is countered by a pervasive fear that social bonds are unraveling, that families are failing to socialize the young, and that crime is making cities virtually uninhabitable. Neither liberals nor conservatives give a convincing account of how to arrest the damage, and the conflict between these blocs obstructs even modest progress, leaving people yet more cynical about what public institutions can accomplish. One result of this widespread distrust of government is the recent defeat of proposals for universal health care. The United States, alone among the industrial democracies, has failed to achieve universal coverage, even as it spends more for health care than any other industrial democracy. Social Darwinism has revived, and the rhetoric of community values, though prevalent, tends to ignore or blame the weakest and most damaged individuals. Irritation and even rage are commonly directed at homeless beggars, welfare mothers, and illegal immigrants.

In its ostensible moment of glory, individualism in the United States is today embattled and shrill. There remains, on the surface, a strong attachment to the value of individual rights — measured, variously, in the prestige of Amnesty International and the continuing power of the National Rifle Association, where the Emersonian ideal of self-reliance has been vulgarized into the demand for a pistol in every bedroom. There is surprisingly little to celebrate now that authentic individualism has succumbed to the Vast Wasteland, paved over by shopping malls and pulverized by mass culture. The virtues of individualism, largely foreclosed in the huge organizations where people work, are left to be celebrated mainly in the realm of consumer choice. The populist version of individualism means access to the Vast Mall and to the innumerable seductive possibilities of mass culture — a compensation for what is missing from the rest of life.

Except in the corridors of that Vast Mall of consumer choice, wide open to anyone who can afford the price of admission, American individualism today primarily takes the form of negation. It's a sour individualism that masks conformity. It echoes the early anti-Federalists in snarling: "Don't tread on me." It knows whom or what it hates better than it knows what kind of world it wants. It cannot imagine a commonality beyond the petty commonality of the tribe. It detests the state more than it affirms any particular positive value beyond production itself. In the arts, individualism worships at the shrine of "creativity." What it produces is largely formula — Disneyism, Barbie, situation comedy, the soul-killing violence of Hollywood. Politically, the rhetoric of individualism has devolved from a vigorous affirmation into an anxious defense against group rights.

The ideals of the "self-made individual" and the "class to end all classes": These were the gods of modernity. Their very extremity was part of their appeal. They were hell-bent for deliverance from illegitimate authority.

They exuded the air of an absolute break with the past. They proposed that individuals make not only themselves but also history. By contrast, other possible ideals of the collective good have been weak, their forms of action vague. Thus, today, the old gods refuse to be buried. The conditions that gave rise to them still hold sway. People are afflicted by terrible inequalities of condition. They do not see why they should have to succumb to their fates. They also seek what they think to be freedom by fleeing it — into protective shelters. The truth is that the old shrines were built for a reason. They weren't only imposed; they were worshipped. Their ruins are still standing.

America's Identity Crisis

It can be dangerous to win. Ideologies, like political alliances, are packed with fuzzy, contradictory ideas; they need to be held together by adversaries. They are tug-of-war teams: When the other team drops the rope and leaves the field, our team falls, too. The collapse of communism and the withering away of the Cold War have generated a certain crisis for the United States. This crisis is intellectual and spiritual, and it is more than North American. It is the problem of the basis for human solidarity.

This is vexing, in particular, for the United States of America, for we were defined, from the beginning, as an unprecedented sort of nation — an idea, or *mirabile dictu*, a dream. For 200 years, the United States proclaimed itself new and enticing. "Americans live in the future," as Ronald Reagan said in 1980. On its utopian side, the country believed that it had not yet formed. It borrowed its energies from the future. This was true for the country as a whole as for the individuals who inhabit it — whence the allure of investment, as powerful for the cab driver and the corner grocer as for the banker. It was true in the (frequently interrupted) commitment to replenish the national energies by welcoming immigrants. It was true in the successive waves of popular demands for social equality made in the name of Americanism itself. Thus did the United States come to understand itself as the homeland of freedom — a tangible place, an incarnation of good that was neither airy like abstract individualism, nor inhuman like international communism.

Dreams are distinctly prone to awakenings. The American awakening has been a rude one, and American confidence is deeply troubled. This is mainly because two endings more or less coincided: the end of the Cold War and the end of prosperity. For almost half a century after World War II, Americans were able to soothe their tensions because the social contract more or less worked. The triumph of 1945 might have spurred an upsurge of class, race, and political tensions but for the coupling of two powerful forces: the economic boom and the coming of the Cold War. Together, they offered quick and emotionally compelling answers to the perennial predicament of American culture or at least ways of staving it off. The Cold War by itself offered a motive for suppressing lingering doubts. Who were we? We were what they were not, what they were trying to crush. They were slavery; we were freedom. They were faceless hordes ruled by faceless bureaucrats and secret police; we were middle-class individualists. The time-honored riddle of American identity evidently had a solution: We Americans were all of us who lined up against them. We were, in fact, the very proof of the commonality of mankind, an *omnium gatherum* of immigrants that had the great virtue of absorbing trivial differences into the common crusade.

Defined most firmly by what we were not, the United States could sustain an appearance, even a conviction, of unity. A strong majority of North Americans could imagine that this was their century, that even if they were not living in luxury, they could be comfortable, and that they too — or at least their children — could find their place in the sun. In the 1950s and 1960s, the United States experienced an extraordinary boost in the standard of living. But the Vietnam war decisively cracked the national identity precisely because it discredited the authorities who had presided over the boom. A growing movement of citizens put to the test the nation's cardinal principle — anti-communism — and found it most specifically murderous. For other reasons as well, in the late 1960s, the prestige of almost all American institutions began to slump. There followed the oil embargo, the decline of the dollar, and (arguably, because of the costs of the Vietnam war) the inflation-fueled trauma of the 1970s. The American boom was over. So was the sense of a shared and robust American destiny.

Although Ronald Reagan was able to regenerate some of the old Cold War religion in the 1980s, the post-World War II foundation of national unity and confidence could not be restored. It was Reagan's political genius to radiate confidence in the American dream along with an intimidating paranoia about the hypothetically menacing Russian bear. His version of economic prosperity involved a massive transfer of wealth upwards in the class system. But the cost of this revived Cold War was too great to permit the Cold War to erase identity puzzlement for long. The $2.5 trillion spent on the military during Reagan's two terms were a major cause of the budget deficits and of other economic imbalances that persist. Economic divisions accentuated racial, ethnic, and other divisions. In the waning days of the Cold War, one began to hear gloomy talk about American decline.

To stabilize a sense of itself, the United States has relied upon a cultural binding that overcomes centrifugal tendencies — not only the self-seeking of individuals but also the group memberships for which Americans have been famous since Tocqueville. Periodically that binding has been nativism. Sometimes, as in the 1960s, the country opens its borders and relaxes; sometimes it shuts down. Every so often, the country has gone into convulsions, tightening its definition of itself: the Alien and Sedition Laws of the 1790s, the Know-Nothing Party of the 1840s, the exclusion of Asians during the latter years of the nineteenth century and the opening decades of the twentieth, the banning of the German language during World War I and the political deportations that followed, the exclusion of Jews during the Holocaust, the McCarthyite fevers of the 1950s. Today, many Californians apparently think they can recover their greatness by building a deeper moat to keep out the "barbarian hordes."

Now, the idea of the United States of America has come unstuck. The binding of the whole is in doubt. A good deal of cultural energy in the United States goes into policing the boundaries of distinct identity groups. Demands for group recognition, just and unjust, absorb more energy than any search for commonalities of identity and belief.

A New Tribal Isolationism

Modern individualism, by itself, is not enough to define a collective identity or a faith in the common destiny of humanity. The movement of individuals in a restless society — and what is modernity if not restless? — tends to become centrifugal. For this reason, there is everywhere a search for cement, for anchorage. Religion is one answer to this search. Nationalism is another, especially with the disbanding of the Soviet empire, like that of the Spanish and Ottoman and Hapsburg empires before it. Many of the current bursts of nationalism differ markedly from the liberal nationalism of nineteenth-century Italians, Hungarians, and Poles. Today's nationalist revivals slip into revenge plays directed by unscrupulous leaders, rationalized by a bitter-end insistence that historical injuries, real or imagined, be answered in kind. The search for historical roots so needed to counter the unmoored restlessness of modernity is perverted into selective memory.

But even in the United States, the quasi-nationalisms of the identity politics of race, sex, gender, ethnicity, and religion are on the rise. Political culture is entranced by difference: difference of identity, interest, history, future. So much so that a pseudo-philosophical name, "postmodernism," has been tagged onto a recognition of differences. To explore the reasons for this upsurge of identity politics would carry us far beyond the scope of this essay. The important point here is that the strength of these tendencies is a function, in large part, of the weaknesses of the commonality ideas of the Enlightenment. The intense feelings that identity politics generate amount to strong reasons why Enlightenment faith is today on the defensive. There is a decomposition into tribes, some defined by blood, others by history, still others by the claim of having transcended blood and history. For the genuflections and passions Americans display on behalf of individual rights today are frequently disingenuous. Recoiling against the spirit of difference, the protests of the tribe of anti-tribalists often have a self-satisfied, conformist, exclusive ring themselves.

The current panic about the fetish of difference, dismissed as "political correctness," is far more than a tempest in an academic teapot. The tribal isolationism of "identity politics" can represent a welling up of dignity, the thrill of a people coming into its own. Certainly the Indian populations of Latin America have need of recognition as they seek to overcome the horrors and humiliations of colonialism. Certainly the long overdue entrance of women into the making of history is a glorious refashioning of the human project. But often, the politics of difference amounts to flights from freedom into the "miracle, mystery, and authority" of the group (to borrow the words of Dostoyevsky's Grand Inquisitor). In the name of consolidating the differences between one group and another, differences within the group are overlooked, diminished, repressed. Frequently, the politics of difference is founded on deep philosophical error: the insistence that people are and must remain incomprehensible to one another, and that what divides people must overwhelm what unites them and what they can understand in common. Today's many secessions from the difficult search for commonality are understandable but deplorable.

To understand the current state of the cultural antagonisms, and the force of the passions that fuel them, is no easy matter, and satire, though welcome, is not always clarifying. Among all the many secessions at work, especially in the United States, those least recognized are the secessions of the relatively affluent. In the eyes of the suburban majority, the city becomes synonymous with crime, drugs, bad schools, and racial conflict. In the United States, the structure of metropolitan government makes it possible for suburbanites to withdraw their taxes from the city, although their affluence depends on urban economic vitality. Both the rich and the not-so-rich withdraw behind literal or figurative gates to be protected by private police forces. They enroll their children in expensive schools. Many of the middle classes, as in Brazil, either live in sequestered fear or aspire to do so. As the resources of the whole republic are segregated, those conditions worsen that lead to middle-class flight in the first place. In these circumstances, talk of the "seamless community" and the "common good" rings hollow.

The high-minded reaction against the politics of difference is often a disappointed liberality of spirit. But often, too, it lapses into a nationalism of blood, soil, and Christ. It is this voice that spoke in the complaint of 1992 Republican presidential hopeful Patrick Buchanan, who frightened a good number of Republicans as well as Democrats when he told the party convention in Houston, "There is a religious war going on in this country, a cultural war as critical to the kind of nation we shall be as the Cold War itself, for this is a war for the soul of America."

This reaction against "secular humanism" and minority demands is itself a politics of tightly drawn boundaries and exclusivist definitions. Within the militant evangelical Christianity that undergirds Buchanan's formulation lies perhaps the most widespread form and certainly the best organized wing of American identity politics. In the voice of the Christian Right, the potentially adhesive force of religion affirms the moral community, but the community it affirms is a community bristling with fortified boundaries. The "West" that it affirms is a permanently embattled, closed and unreconstructed West. In the eyes of many so-called cultural conservatives, the community to be affirmed is itself restrictive, itself secessionist. What is to be conserved is evidently a fortress from which the cultural upheavals of the 1960s can, in theory, be rolled back: a community in which women best remain at home, homosexuality is a sin, abortion is murder, prayer belongs in the public schools, and taxes should subsidize the private schools. These so-called conservatives are willfully blind to the ways in which uncontrolled capital is one of the prime forces of cultural destabilization. For example, forcing women to work, regardless of their preferences, because the decline in wages relative to the standard of living has reduced the single-earner family to the status of a fossil.

Multiculturalism has been proposed as an ideology for the future of the United States. Yet multiculturalism is not so much an ideology as a fact susceptible to a multitude of understandings. The question is not whether to acknowledge the fact that the white majority is shrinking (though at a rate that is frequently exaggerated). There is no disputing that some 90 percent of immigrants to the United States today come from Latin America, Asia, and Africa. The fastest-growing demographic category is composed of the children of mixed-race marriages. There is a coloring of the United States. The question is, What does this mean?

The important questions are questions of value, and they are inter-locked: What shall we make of the indisputable facts of demographic upheaval? What do they leave out? Do they suffice as a framework for political and cultural life? And what becomes of the universalist hope and faith? One need not succumb to the moral panic displayed by conservatives sounding alarms about multiculturalism, often distorting the facts of university life in the process. One need not go nearly that far to be concerned about the cross-cultural bonds that are weakening, the quarrels that are absorbing social energy sorely needed elsewhere. One need not fear that the horrors of Beirut or Bosnia await us in New York or Los Angeles to worry about the twilight of common dreams. One need not believe the fairy tale that America is a classless society, or has ever been; one need not believe that the dream was universally accessible; one need not deny the reality of white and male supremacy, or the many oppressions in American history, to recognize the virtues in Benjamin Franklin's formulation about his fellow American revolu-tionaries that they would "all hang together or assuredly...all hang separately."

Reviving the Democratic Faith

I have mentioned the most powerful worldly forces subverting the possibility of a decent life and a common dream. Doing so, I align myself with the liberals, socialists, and unclassifiable intellectuals who resist the onward march of identity politics — not simply in the name of conserving some vanished republicanism, but in the name of reason, an ecumenical spirit, and a longed-for resumption of Enlightenment faith. The ranks of this open universalism are thin today in the United States, in part out of misplaced guilt and a reluctance to be seen as siding with conservatives. Where once it was the party of difference that was silenced, today it is the party of commonality that silences itself.

This party of commonality seeks an open universalism, not a nostalgia for the exclusive and fraudulent universalist claims of the past, but a double commitment:

First, there must be an insistence on the irreducible value of reason. I do not mean reason severed from feeling or from a recognition of distinct and diverse perspectives. I mean a reason to which everyone can appeal while honoring the life of feeling, tracing distinct histories, refining perspectives. Why not recognize that such progress as has taken place against slavery, exploitation, violence against women and children, has taken place in the name of universalist principles — "all men are created equal" — and in the direction of the expansion of the categories of "men" to include all humanity? Why not recognize that it is indispensable to appeal to a reason that can be grasped and shared and spread across the lines of different experience and identity? (Indeed, when it suits them, the partisans of identity politics themselves resort to canons of argument, or caricatures of argument, complete with parodies of evidence. Even the scurrilous anti-Semitic tract published by Louis Farrakhan's Nation of Islam, "The Secret Relationship of Blacks and Jews," which idiotically maintains that Jews ran the slave trade without mentioning Christians, includes footnotes in its caricature of scholarship.)

Second, in political life, we badly need mutual recognitions. As historians of race and gender have shown, the differences that societies recognize change throughout history. Homosexual desires and pigmentations may be inborn, but the category of "the homosexual" or "the mulatto" is made, not born. A recognition of these fluctuations might make for a certain humility. Moreover, the elements of a decent life — food, clothing, shelter — vary relatively little. Distinct habits of thought and experience are accessible to those whose thought and experience are different. Communication among peoples, tribes, interests, and individuals is feasible even if only "up to a point," but certainly up to that point. An open universalism entails a commitment to conversation across boundaries — conversation predicated on the existence of a common nature, eager to find points of contact as well as to clarify difference, eager to sympathize, translate, explain.

In short, we need a revival of democratic faith — of, by, and for the entire *demos*. We need to respect difference without ceasing to cultivate commonality. We need to build up public institutions that cross the barriers of difference — public schools, public spaces, shared culture, government bodies, and political coalitions. And how is such a revival possible without the overcoming of race and class barriers? What is required are challenges to unjust monopolies of power, but what is also required of everyone is a certain generosity. Above all, the privileged need to commit themselves to remedy the most bitter exclusions: those of poverty. While identity politicians have been striving to get greater representation for their constituencies, the subject of poverty and class has virtually disappeared from the political lexicon of the United States. This is a scandal.

We also badly need a shared ecological commitment. We live in one world, in one greenhouse, under one ozone layer. Greens from the professional classes need to recognize that the dangers to public health from headlong industrial development fall disproportionately on the working classes, who often labor in vile factories and live in neighborhoods more likely to be the sites of toxic dumps and poisoned air than the neighborhoods of the rich. The same obviously applies on a global scale.

Throughout the wealthier nations, there is a need to shift energy and intelligence from the refining of differences to the composing of majorities. We do not need a political culture that rhapsodizes about marginality. In particular, it is long overdue to stop cherishing apocalyptic and absolutist thinking about the glories of race, class, or gender. Let us empty the echo chambers of revolutionary fantasy. Let those who are properly committed to the poor cease trying to reconstitute Marxism the way followers of Ptolemy in the seventeenth century strained to preserve their antiquated paradigm by making it denser with "epicycles."

Too many people have busied themselves digging trenches to fortify their borders, lining those trenches with postmodern insulation, and scrambling for cover in their hardened identity bunkers. Enough bunkers! What we ought to be building are bridges.

Chapter 9

The Twenty-First Century Betwixt Us

Sergio Ramírez

Today, the ideology determining the fate of political and social systems in the aftermath of the Cold War resembles the intellectual machinery of the Enlightenment, which first informed a benevolent despotism and later a number of liberal revolutions: in both cases, the concepts have been contrived in places far from Latin America. And like the changes in the economy and the market which arose during the Industrial Revolution, the changes of post-modernity, as we enter the twenty-first century, are being developed elsewhere.

This is due to a persistent division of ideological labor which aims to define, from the centers of global power, what models and systems of universal application will be decided. In this way, we can also see the differences between the first and third worlds, regardless of ideological or cultural models, whether they be Rousseau, Marx, Spengler, or Fukuyama.

The effects of a change are nonetheless visible, and they produce real alterations, though disorganized and belated and very often inefficient in terms of transformation and progress. The liberal revolutions of Latin America were the consequence of a necessity, but they were also the result of the acritical importation of an entire ideological system, as would later occur with Marxist notions regarding history and society and Leninist ideas with respect to the state.

The thesis concerning the end of history, and the end of ideologies themselves, as championed by Francis Fukuyama, may well be ephemeral as a *fin-de-siecle* proposal linked to the disappearance of a bipolar world and the end of the Cold War. It is a dictum, however, that has helped to consolidate neoliberal models adopted once again in an acritical manner.

I say "once again" because, from its foundation in the nineteenth century, Latin American capitalism aimed to copy Europe's ideological inspirations with regard to development, national integration, territorial conquest, free trade, and white immigrations, so that progress would prosper according to the liberal construct as represented by Domingo Faustino Sarmiento in *Facundo: civilización y barbarie*.

Translated by Roberto Tejada.

More recently, Latin American socialism also tried to copy another intellectual framework from Europe, engendered as a counterpoint to the Industrial Revolution. Marxism was imported and disseminated as a way of ideologically effecting a change of power on the part of the working classes, a philosophy of inevitable results that aimed to inaugurate the beginning of history, as today some speak of the end of history.

Both liberalism and Marxism were transplanted in Latin America as panaceas that promised to alter reality and to produce effects of change. While both systems have been practiced in different regions, neither model has been successful. Following independence, liberalism managed to dominate notions regarding the real organization of political systems, economy and the market.

In Latin America, Marxism-Leninism was never more than a constant challenge to the liberal system — with the exception of Cuba where the state is organized following that model. It began with the workers' movement to later include popular fronts, leftist parties, and finally the armed struggle which by mid-century proved to be a challenge as well to the traditional left.

With the end of a bipolar world — and, as a consequence, with the end of the Cold War — the old rules of nineteenth-century liberalism have returned as guiding principles of a modernity raised over the ruins of real socialism. While a planned economy (state initiative versus private initiative) had posed a challenge to the market, that challenge is now defunct and so is the idea of the state to which this economy gave origin.

With the end of the Cold War, neoliberalism represents an ideological agreement within the context of contemporary economic relations, though it pretends to be different in nature to that of the nineteenth century. The ideological concepts of classic liberalism are no different, however, even if we see them emerging above the rubble of classic socialism.

Real liberalism has been imposed over real socialism; universal opinion believes that modernity equals neoliberalism, and real socialism is obsolete. The fall of the latter has, in geopolitical terms, put an end to a dispute that has lasted throughout most of the century.

The end of the bipolar world, however, coincides with a crisis regarding this same liberal model in Latin American countries — a crisis marked by an exhausted economic system, accelerated hyperinflation, the draining of capital, and the excessive burden of foreign debt. As a result, emphasis is placed on the economic model, more than on the political model, because authoritarianism, whether from the right or from the left, is rapidly losing prestige, and no one dares to offer it as an alternative.

Furthermore, the confirmation (or ideological resurrection) of the liberal model links the market to classic democracy, a concept that demands revision. The end of the Cold War has erased the threatening allegations aimed at democratic systems which, paradoxically, had allowed military dictatorships and restricted or low-intensity democracies compatible with the market to be established in the name of national security — a further paradox, because the market, in terms of doctrine, has been linked to freedom.

The neoliberal option acquires the nature of a philosophy. Decades before, the socialist model of power to achieve changes in structures was proposed by political leaders, armed or unarmed, as a condition of modernization. Today, neoliberalism is proposed as the paradigm free of all challenges by economists who in their turn have become the new philosophers of history, again a condition of modernization.

The proposals of this new modernity have been adopted in an acritical manner by certain Latin American governments, while others have been forced to put these proposals into practice. Neoliberal philosophy is strictly derived from the economy, expressed through adjusted monetary programs that measure the possibility and the opportunity for development in terms of discipline. Once again, they are the fruit of a necessity, but at the same time, they are also the result of an external ideological imposition. And this confirms, once again, the old pattern with regard to the acritical importation of models.

Neoliberal philosophy demands that the market be restored all its lost privileges. It also makes several other claims: a reduced or marginal role of the state in the economy, the inflexible adjustment of public spending, out-and-out privatization, and the payment of a renegotiated foreign debt. There is no other available pattern of development for international financial organisms, for they impose the stipulated rules and supervise their strict enforcement.

I believe we are facing the greatest challenge that the left has had to confront in Latin America. It is yet to be seen whether the left is capable of presenting alternative models (not a monolithic model but rather several models) that are viable and credible and whose point of departure is, for the first time, a critical perception of reality and of the need for change. Facing the model of neoliberalism, the left will have to demonstrate whether it can offer the models of a neosocialism — models, I should add, that do not repeat the old authoritarian notions of socialism the way neoliberalism repeats the original conception of liberalism.

One substantial reason why the Latin American left became obsolete was its antagonism toward democracy and its arbitrary distinction between a proletariat democracy and a bourgeois democracy. Far from democracy itself, that proposal wasted time in revising the global concept of democracy, so as to retrieve it from its classic mold. The Leninist notion that a historical project of social change could only come about from the total centralization of power, in the hands of a single party, had few real effects. Furthermore, in a debate which lasted decades, it resulted in a lack of trust and prestige with regard to the ideological initiative of the left.

A renovating proposal from the left must seek creative responses to the issue of democracy, which as a tool of neoliberal doctrine can often prove to be more restrictive than revitalized. Moreover, the integral renovation of democracy, with real unrestricted areas for participation, can perhaps yield a different kind of economy which also features room for plural participation.

This is where the profound revision of the concept of democracy must face reality. After almost two centuries, the liberal model has assumed the layered stratification of Latin American societies, as if it were a geological sampling. There has always been a coexistence among different economic systems and between different standards of social well-being which correspond to different historical states, from the most primitive to the most modern.

In Latin America, democracy cannot restrict itself to assuring participation from the most modernized sectors — the middle and educated classes. It must serve as an instrument of modernization for society as a whole, beginning with the most underprivileged and marginal sectors which have yet to enjoy the benefits of civilization. Global participation must follow the two-way route of action in economic life as well as action in political and social life.

Democracy, therefore, must be adopted without the slightest reservation. The aim of democracy should be to work through its institutions, to fortify the condition of rights, and to function in its representative capacity. It should also gain force in its participatory manifestation — community and class, unions and guilds. It should multiply the spaces for opinion and information, and it should not promote the concept of a civil society reserved for the middle classes; it should include both the working classes and the marginal sectors of society. It should be a democracy that is both urban and rural.

The idea is not to propose, once again, a "popular" democracy — which is already a semantic redundancy, for all power from the people is popular — but rather to posit an integral democracy which permits a daily, plural participation at all levels of society, including its electoral system.

Gone is the heroic era which conceived power at the service of an historical project of total transformation. Hence, the total political model sheltered by that project is no longer expedient. The authoritarian model of the right is now obsolete and irretrievable, for it has been buried along with the bipolar confrontation.

There is no other point of encounter, therefore, but through the democratic system, both unrestricted and dynamic as it tests the viability of a sustainable long-term development, which can be organized beyond political or ideological contingencies on national or transnational terms. We must forge this space for a common participation.

A proposal from the left must replace the neoliberal model with alternatives which are removed from populism. It will be necessary seriously to face the problems of stability and economic development, within a perspective of compromise that excludes no one.

This does not mean tolerating the market on ideological terms. It means using the market as an efficient tool for achieving economic transformation, generating wealth that will benefit all of society according to the laws of a new equity. This is the only way of taking on the challenge of modernity and of becoming the creators of modernity.

Equity in the distribution of wealth was always a missing factor in the classic conception of liberalism, and it is far from being an essential point in the neoliberal platform. In its proposal for modernity, the left must make distributive justice an essential economic goal, as it should protect our natural resources and the environment, so as to achieve the concept of sustainable development.

The problems regarding poverty and marginalization have not been solved by liberalism in over two centuries. There is no reason to believe that neoliberalism will achieve this now — for the very reason that it readopts the former rules of the game. Marginalization continues to increase, and poverty grows more offensive by the day. It is difficult to speak of modernity facing the continued reality of underdevelopment, infant death rate, poor health conditions, unemployment, and ecological depletion, all of which constitute a heavy burden.

The structures created in Latin America as of independence are now obsolete, and their most negative effects have been to impede the global modernization of our societies. I am not implying structuralist budgets. If we accept democracy as a dynamic factor of social mobility and as an integral concept, we must also accept that economic democracy imposes an alteration of structures, especially if we speak in terms of modernity and modernization. And these are obsolete structures, even in terms of the market.

Over the last two centuries, the gaps separating the countries of Latin America from the first world have not been breached. It is hardly a commonplace to insist on the fact that the injustice of international economic relations is, today more than ever, an unbearable burden for our economies to shoulder, economies that are weakened with each new effort.

As far as global integration is concerned, we cannot circumvent the challenge whereby the countries of Latin America truly consent, in an integral way, to participate in the postmodern economy and in the benefits of technology. In practice, the neoliberal model may well begin to lose many of its most aggressive ideological aspects, but the market economy will continue to gain strength as both the internal relations of each country and international relations are defined.

Market ideology (free trade or free initiative) emerged with the republican institutions of Latin America during independence, but it did not resolve the problem of integral development — one that would be capable of transforming Latin America into leading countries, into producers of technology and of technological goods — nor has it resolved the problem to date.

The ideology of free trade or free initiative has since served to define international economic relations, but from a first-world perspective, Latin America's initiatives were subject to the very force of the market that assigned roles in the international division of labor.

For decades, these relations helped to stratify the internal structures of Latin American countries, and subsequently they contributed to injustice. If both these internal and external relations fail to change, democracy, bereft of justice and well-being, will once again become a precarious dream.

This is why, from the perspective of underprivileged countries such as those of Latin America, neoliberalism — more than just an instrument of modernization and of postmodernity itself — is now obsolete, as obsolete as the model of real socialism over which it sings its victory.

Latin America has not exactly been invited to the banquet of postmodernity, just as it was never invited during the nineteenth century — for there also existed a sort of postmodernism at the time. At any rate, we will have to make room for ourselves among the guests, as we demand a modification in the economic relations that postmodernity fails thoroughly to change.

Postmodernism will prove to be of little use to Latin America if the tendency is to repeat the old story where, as in the past, we find ourselves dining in the kitchen, listening at a distance to the voices and clamor of the feast. We must revert this tendency in two ways so that our countries can find themselves in the position of entering postmodernity by breaching both the internal and external gaps in a new kind of relationship with the first world.

In the contemporary world, national patterns of development will necessarily have to admit the hardships involved in the patterns of integration as a factor of viability with regard to internal growth, and the larger market systems will increasingly influence local markets.

All this is true. Nevertheless, first-world countries will have to demonstrate that integration is possible on equitable terms, so as to erase the old prejudices — still prevalent to date — regarding inequality and injustice in international relations.

The true test of postmodernity vis-à-vis Latin America will take place in Mexico. The North American Free Trade Agreement (NAFTA) integrates a second-world country — one that typifies the unbalanced development in internal economic relations — with two first-world countries, one of which is none other than the United States.

NAFTA will be the real stage for a three-sided transference, in economic, social, technological, and cultural terms, and it must demonstrate that it is also the stage for relations based on justice and whose most visible effects should be the growth of well-being among Mexicans and the integral modernization of Mexico. Otherwise, it will be regarded as a failure by all countries in Latin America, and the macro-patterns of integration will lose all credibility among us.

It is imperative to note as well that the classical notion of nation state will begin to change rapidly with the phenomena of integrated markets and global communication. This presents us with another challenge: we must prevent the risks of having our national identities weakened by increasing transnationalization and must forge new concepts with regard to identity and sovereignty.

Postmodernity modifies the classic notions regarding the nation state, as we are witnessing now in Europe with the Maastricht Treaty, which is a superior form of collective organization. At the same time, however, nationalisms based on racial and religious prejudices have begun to appear around the world in extremely inflamed battles.

For Latin Americans, nationalism has a beneficial potential which we should add to the desirable elements of modernization. Our common national features, and our various forms of nationalism, have been constructed over centuries and ought to be preserved and defended, not to make tradition a hindrance but to lend substance to modernity.

The greatest challenge posed to a change in (or a modernization of) nationalist concepts will occur within the context of NAFTA in Mexico — Latin America's archetype of a nationalistic country and one which has represented the limits of the most visible contention in the political conflict between Latin America and the United States.

Here, then, is yet another challenge facing Latin America. In terms of a global modernization, we must make integration work without debilitating our national identity.

Section III

A New World Culture?

Chapter 10

Reflections: Mexico and the United States

Octavio Paz

When I was in India, witnessing the never-ending quarrels between Hindus and Muslims, I asked myself more than once this question: What accident or misfortune of history caused two religions so obviously irreconcilable as Hinduism and Muhammadanism to coexist in the same society? The presence of the purest and most intransigent form of monotheism in the bosom of a civilization that has elaborated the most complex polytheism seemed to me a verification of the indifference with which history perpetrates its paradoxes. And yet I could hardly be surprised at the contradictory presence in India of Hinduism and Muhammadanism. How could I forget that I myself, as a Mexican, was (and am) part of a no less singular paradox — that of Mexico and the United States?

Our countries are neighbors, condemned to live alongside each other; they are separated, however, more by profound social, economic, and psychic differences than by physical and political frontiers. These differences are self-evident, and a superficial glance might reduce them to the well-known opposition between development and underdevelopment, wealth and poverty, power and weakness, domination and dependence. But the really fundamental difference is an invisible one, and in addition it is perhaps insuperable.

To prove that it has nothing to do with economics or political power, we have only to imagine a Mexico suddenly turned into a prosperous, mighty country, a superpower like the United States. Far from disappearing, the difference would become more acute and more clear-cut. The reason is obvious: We are two distinct versions of Western civilization.

Ever since we Mexicans began to be aware of national identity — in about the middle of the eighteenth century — we have been interested in our

This is a slightly abridged version of "Reflections: The United States and Mexico," by Octavio Paz, from *The New Yorker*, September 17, 1979. Reprinted by permission; © 1979. English translation by Rachel Phillips, originally in *The New Yorker*.

northern neighbors. First, with a mixture of curiosity and disdain; later on with an admiration and enthusiasm that were soon tinged with fear and envy. The idea the Mexican people have of the United States is contradictory, emotional, and impervious to criticism; it is a mythic image. The same can be said of the vision of our intellectuals and writers.

Something similar happens with Americans, be they writers or politicians, businessmen or only travellers. I am not forgetting the existence of a small number of remarkable studies by various American specialists, especially in the field of archeology and ancient and modern Mexican history. The perceptions of the American novelists and poets who have written on Mexican themes have often been brilliant, but they have also been fragmentary.

In general, Americans have not looked for Mexico in Mexico; they have looked for their obsessions, enthusiasms, phobias, hopes, interests — and these are what they have found. In short, the history of a mutual and stubborn deceit, usually involuntary though not always so.

Of course, the differences between Mexico and the United States are not imaginary projections but objective realities. Some are quantitative and can be explained by the social, economic, and historical development of the two countries. The more permanent ones, though also the result of history, are not easily definable or measurable. I have pointed out that they belong to the realm of civilization, that fluid zone of imprecise contours in which are fused and confused ideas and beliefs, institutions and technologies, styles and morals, fashions and churches, the material culture and that evasive reality which we rather inaccurately call *le génie des peuples*. The reality to which we give the name of the civilization does not allow of easy definition. It is each society's vision of the world and also its feeling about time; there are nations that are hurrying toward the future, and others whose eyes are fixed on the past. Civilization is a society's style, its way of living and dying. It embraces the erotic and the culinary arts; dancing and burial; courtesy and curses; work and leisure; rituals and festivals; punishments and rewards; dealings with the dead and rewards; dealings with the dead and with the ghosts who people our dreams; attitudes toward women and children, old people and strangers, enemies and allies; eternity and the present; the here and now and the beyond. A civilization is not only a system of values but a world of forms and codes of behavior, rules and exceptions. It is society's visible side — institutions, monuments, works, things — but it is especially its submerged, invisible side: beliefs, desires, fears, repressions, dreams.

The points of the compass have served to locate us in history as well as in space. The East-West duality soon acquired a more symbolic than geographical significance, and became an emblem of the opposition between civilizations. The East-West opposition has always been considered basic and primordial; it alludes to the movement of the sun, and is therefore an image of the direction and meaning of our living and dying. The East-West relationship symbolizes two directions, two attitudes, two civilizations. The North-South duality refers more to the opposition between different ways of life and different sensibilities. The contrasts between North and South can be oppositions within the same civilization.

Clearly, the opposition between Mexico and the United States belongs to the North-South duality as much from the geographical as the symbolic point of view. It is an ancient opposition which was already unfolding in pre-Columbian America, so that it antedates the very existence of the United States and Mexico. The northern part of the continent was settled by nomadic, warrior nations; Mesoamerica, on the other hand, was the home of an agricultural civilization, with complex social and political institutions, dominated by warlike theocracies that invented refined and cruel rituals, great art, and vast cosmogonies inspired by a very original vision of time. The great opposition of pre-Columbian America — all that now includes the United States and Mexico — was between different ways of life: nomads and settled peoples, hunters and farmers. This division greatly influenced the later development of the United States and Mexico. The policies of the English and the Spanish toward the Indians were in large part determined by this division; it was not insignificant that the former established themselves in the territory of the nomads and the latter in that of the settled peoples.

The differences between the English and the Spaniards who founded New England and New Spain were no less decisive than those that separated the nomadic from the settled Indians. Again, it was an opposition within the same civilization. Just as the American Indians' world view and beliefs sprang from a common source, irrespective of their ways of life, so Spanish and English shared the same intellectual and technical culture. And the opposition between them, though of a different sort, was as deep as that dividing and Aztec from an Iroquois. And so the new opposition between English and Spaniards was grafted onto the old opposition between nomadic and settled peoples. The distinct and divergent attitudes of Spaniards and English have often been described before. All of them can be summed up in one fundamental difference, in which perhaps the dissimilar evolution of Mexico and the United States originated: in England the Reformation triumphed, whereas Spain was the champion of the Counter-Reformation.

As we all know, the reformist movement in England had political consequences that were decisive in the development of Anglo-Saxon democracy. In Spain, evolution went in the opposite direction. Once the resistance of the last Muslim was crushed, Spain achieved a precarious political — but not national — unity by means of dynastic alliances. At the same time, the monarchy suppressed regional autonomies and municipal freedoms, closing off the possibility of eventual evolution into a modern democracy. Lastly, Spain was deeply marked by Arab domination, and kept alive the notion of crusade and holy war, which it had inherited from Christian and Muslim alike. In Spain, the traits of the modern era, which was just beginning, and of the old society coexisted but never blended completely. The contrast with England could not be sharper. The history of Spain and her former colonies, from the sixteenth century onward, is the history of an ambiguous approach — attraction and repulsion — to the modern era.

The discovery and conquest of America are events that inaugurated modern world history, but Spain and Portugal carried them out with the sensibility and tenor of the Reconquest. Nothing more original occurred to Cortes's soldiers, amazed by the pyramids and temples of the Mayans and

Aztecs, than to compare them with the mosques of Islam. Conquest and evangelization: these two words, deeply Spanish and Catholic, are also deeply Muslim. Conquest means not only the occupation of foreign territories and the subjugation of their inhabitants but also the conversion of the conquered. The conversion legitimized the conquest. This politico-religious philosophy was diametrically opposed to that of English colonizing; the idea of evangelization occupied a secondary place in England's colonial expansion.

The Christianity brought to Mexico by the Spaniards was the syncretic Catholicism of Rome, which had assimilated the pagan gods, turning them into saints and devils. The phenomenon was repeated in Mexico: the idols were baptized, and in popular Mexican Catholicism the old beliefs and divinities are still present, barely hidden under a veneer of Christianity. Not only the popular religion of Mexico but the Mexicans' entire life is steeped in Indian culture — the family, love, friendship, attitudes toward one's father and mother, popular legends, the forms of civility and life in common, the image of authority and political power, the vision of death and sex, work and festivity. Mexico is the most Spanish country in Latin America; at the same time it is the most Indian. Mesoamerican civilization died a violent death, but Mexico is Mexico thanks to the Indian presence. Though the language and the religion, the political institutions and the culture of the country are Western, there is one aspect of Mexico that faces in another direction — the Indian direction. Mexico is a nation between two civilizations and two pasts.

In the United States, the Indian element does not appear. This, is my opinion, is the major difference between our two countries. The Indians who were not exterminated were corralled in "reservations." The Christian horror of "fallen nature" extended to the natives of America: the United States was founded on a land without a past. The historical memory of Americans is European, not American. For this reason, one of the most powerful and persistent themes in American literature, from Whitman to William Carlos Williams and from Melville to Faulkner, has been the search for (or invention of) American roots. We owe some of the major works of the modern era to this desire for incarnation, this obsessive need to be rooted in American soil.

Exactly the opposite is true of Mexico, land of superimposed pasts. Mexico City was built on the ruins of Tenochtitlán, the Aztec city that was built in the likeness of Tula, the Toltec city that was built in the likeness of Teotihuacán, the first great city on the American continent. Every Mexican bears within him this continuity, which goes back two thousand years. It doesn't matter that this presence is almost always unconscious and assumes the naive forms of legend and even superstition. It is not something known but something lived. The Indian presence means that one of the facets of Mexican culture is not Western. Is there anything like this in the United States? Each of the ethnic groups making up the multiracial democracy that is the United States has its own culture and tradition, and some of them — the Chinese and the Japanese, for example — are not Western. These traditions exist alongside the dominant American tradition without becoming one with it. They are foreign bodies within American culture. In some cases, the most notable being that of the Chicanos, the minorities defend their traditions against or in the face of the American tradition. The Chicanos' resistance is cultural as well as political and social.

If the different attitudes of Hispanic Catholicism and English Protestant-ism could be summed up in two words, I would say that the Spanish attitude is inclusive and the English exclusive. In the former, the notions of conquest and domination are bound up with ideas of conversion and assimilation; in the latter, conquest and domination imply not the conversion of the conquered but segregation. An inclusive society, founded on the double principle of domination and conversion, is bound to be hierarchical, centralist, and respectful of the individual characteristics of each group. It believes in the strict division of classes and groups, each one governed by special laws and statutes, but all embracing the same faith and obeying the same lord. An exclusive society is bound to cut itself off from the natives, either by physical exclusion or by extermination; at the same time, since each community of pure-minded men is isolated from other communities, it tends to treat its members as equals and to assure the autonomy and freedom of each group of believers. The origins of American democracy are religious, and in the early communities of New England that dual, contradictory tension between freedom and equality which has been the leitmotiv of the history of the United States was already present.

The opposition that I have just outlined is expressed with great clarity in two religious terms: "communion" and "purity." This opposition pro-foundly affects attitudes toward work, festivity, the body, and death. For the society of New Spain, work did not redeem, and had no value in itself. Manual work was servile. The superior man neither worked nor traded. He made war, he commanded, he legislated. He also thought, contemplated, wooed, loved, and enjoyed himself. Leisure was noble. Work was good because it produced wealth, but wealth was good because it was intended to be spent — to be consumed in those holocausts called war, in the construction of temples and palaces, in pomp and festivity. The dissipation of wealth took different forms: gold shone on the altars or was poured out in celebration. Even today in Mexico, at least in the small cities and towns, work is the precursor of the fiesta. The year revolves on the double axis of work and festival, saving and spending. The fiesta is sumptuous and intense, lively and funereal; it is a vital, multicolored frenzy that evaporates in smoke, ashes, nothingness. In the aesthetics of perdition, the fiesta is the lodging place of death.

The United States has not really known the art of the festival, except in the last few years, with the triumph of hedonism over the old Protestant ethnic. This is natural. A society that so energetically affirmed the redemptive value of work could not help chastising as depraved the cult of the festival and the passion for spending. The Protestant rejection was inspired by religion rather than economics. The Puritan conscience could not see that the value of the festival was actually a religious value: communion. In the festival, the orgiastic element is central; it marks a return to the beginning, to the primordial state in which each one is united with the great all. Every true festival is communion. Here the opposition between communion and purity is clear. For the Puritans and their heirs, work is redemptive because it frees man, and this liberation is a sign of God's choice. Work is purification, which is also a separation: the chosen one ascends, breaks the bonds binding him to earth, which are the laws of his fallen nature. For the Mexicans, communion represents exactly the opposite: not separation but participation, not breaking away but joining together; the great universal commixture, the great bathing in the waters of the beginning, a state beyond purity and impurity.

In Christianity, the body's status is inferior. But the body is an always active force, and its explosions can destroy a civilization. Doubtless for this reason, the church from the start made a pact with the body. If the Church did not restore the body to the place it occupied in Greco-Roman society, it did try to give the body back its dignity: the body is fallen nature, but in itself it is innocent. After all, Christianity, unlike Buddhism, say, is the worship of an incarnate god. The dogma of the resurrection of the dead dates from the time of primitive Christianity; the cult of the Virgin appeared later, in the Middle Ages. Both beliefs are the highest expressions of this urge for incarnation, which typifies Christian spirituality. Both came to Mesoamerica with Spanish culture, and were immediately fused, the former with the funeral worship of the Indians, the latter with the worship of the goddesses of fertility and war.

The Mexicans' vision of death which is also the hope of resurrection, is as profoundly steeped in Catholic eschatology as in Indian naturalism. The Mexican death is of the body, exactly the opposite of the American death, which is abstract and disembodied. For Mexicans, death sees and touches itself; it is the body emptied of the soul, the pile of bones that somehow, as in the Aztec poem, must bloom again. For Americans, death is what is not seen: absence, the disappearance of the person. In the Puritan consciousness, death was always present, but as a moral entity, an idea. Later on, scientism pushed death out of the American consciousness. Death melted away and became unmentionable. Finally, in vast segments of the American population of today, progressive rationalism and idealism have been replaced by neo-hedonism. But the cult of the body and of pleasure implies the recognition and acceptance of death. The body is mortal, and the kingdom of pleasure is that of the moment, as Epicurus saw better than anyone else. American hedonism closes its eyes to death, and has been incapable of exorcising the destructive power of the moment with a wisdom like that of the Epicureans of antiquity. Present-day hedonism is the last recourse of the anguished and the desperate, and expression of the nihilism that is eroding the West.

Capitalism exalts the activities and behavior patterns traditionally called virile: aggressiveness, the spirit of competition and emulation, combativeness. American society made these values its own. This perhaps explains why nothing like the Mexicans' devotion to the Virgin of Guadalupe appears in the different versions of Christianity professed by Americans, including the Catholic minority. The Virgin unites the religious sensibilities of the Mediterranean and Mesoamerica, both of them regions that fostered ancient cults of feminine divinities. Guadalupe-Tonantzin is the mother of all Mexicans — Indians, mestizos, whites — but she is also a warrior virgin whose image has often appeared on the banners of peasant uprisings. In the Virgin of Guadalupe we encounter a very ancient vision of femininity which, as was true of the pagan goddesses, is not without a heroic tint.

When I talk about the masculinity of the American capitalist society, I am not unaware that American women have gained rights and posts still denied elsewhere. But they have obtained them as "subjects under the law"; that is to say, as neuter or abstract entities, as citizens, not as woman. Now, I believe that much as our civilization needs equal rights for men and women, it also needs a feminization, like the one that courtly love brought about in the outlook of medieval Europe. Or like the feminine irradiation that the Virgin of Guadalupe casts on the imagination and sensibility of us Mexicans. Because of the Mexican woman's Hispano-Arabic and Indian heritage, her social situation is deplorable, but what I want to emphasize here is not so much the nature of the relation between men and women as the intimate relationship of woman with those elusive symbols which we call femininity and masculinity. For the reasons I noted earlier, Mexican women have a very lively awareness of the body. For them, the body, woman's and man's, is a concrete, palpable reality. Not an abstraction or a function but an ambiguous magnetic force, in which pleasure and pain, fertility and death are inextricably intertwined.

Pre-Columbian Mexico was a mosaic of nations, tribes, and languages. For its part, Spain was also a conglomeration of nations and races, even though it had realized political unity. The heterogeneity of Mexican society was the other face of Spanish centralism. The political centralism of the Spanish monarchy had religious orthodoxy as its complement, and even as its foundation. The true, effective unity of Mexican society has been brought about slowly over several centuries, but its political and religious unity was decreed from above as the joint expression of the Spanish monarchy and the Catholic Church. Mexico had a state and a church before it was a nation. In this respect also, Mexico's evolution has been very different from that of the United States, where the small colonial communities had from their inception a clear-cut and belligerent concept of their identity as regards the state. For North Americans, the nation antedated the state.

Another difference: In those small colonial communities, a fusion had taken place among religious convictions, the embryonic national consciousness, and political institutions. So harmony, not contradiction, existed between the North American's religious convictions and their democratic institutions; whereas in Mexico Catholicism was identified with the viceregal regime, and was its orthodoxy. Therefore, when, after independence, the Mexican liberals tried to implant democratic institutions, they had to confront the Catholic Church. The establishment of a republican democracy in Mexico meant a radical break with the past, and led to the civil wars of the nineteenth century. These wars produced the militarism that, in turn, produced the dictatorship of Porfirio Díaz. The liberals defeated the Church, but they could not implant true democracy — only an authoritarian regime wearing democracy's mask.

A no less profound difference was the opposition between Catholic orthodoxy and Protestant reformism. In Mexico, Catholic orthodoxy had the philosophical form of Neo-Thomism, a mode of thought more apologetic than critical, and defensive in the face of the emerging modernity. Orthodoxy prevented examination and criticism. In New England, the communities were often made up of religious dissidents or, at least, of people who believed that the Scriptures should be read freely. On one side, orthodoxy, dogmatic philosophy, and the cult of authority. On the other, reading and free interpretation of the doctrine. Both societies were religious, but their religious attitudes were irreconcilable. I am not thinking only of dogmas and principles but of the very ways in which the two societies practiced and understood religion. One society fostered the complex and majestic conceptual structure of orthodoxy, an equally complex ecclesiastical hierarchy, wealthy and militant religious orders, and a ritualistic view of religion, in which the sacraments occupied a central place. The other fostered free discussion of the Scriptures, a small and often a poor clergy, a tendency to eliminate the hierarchical boundaries between the simple believer and the priest, and a religious practice based not on ritual but on ethics, and not on the sacraments but on the internalizing of faith.

If one considers the historical evolution of the two societies, the main difference seems to be the following: the modern world began with the Reformation, which was the religious criticism of religion and the necessary antecedent of the Enlightenment; with the Counter-Reformation and New-Thomism, Spain and her possessions closed themselves to the modern world. They had no Enlightenment, because they had neither a Reformation nor an intellectual religious movement like Jansenism. And so, though Spanish-American civilization is to be admired on many counts, it reminds one of a structure of great solidity — at once convent, fortress, and palace — built to last, not to change. In the long run, that construction became a confine, a prison. The United States was born of the Reformation and the Enlightenment. It came into being under the sign of criticism and self-criticism. Now, when one talks of criticism one is talking of change. The transformation of critical philosophy into progressive ideology came about and reached its peak in the nineteenth century. The broom of rationalist criticism swept the ideological sky clean of myths and beliefs; the ideology of progress, in its turn, displaced the timeless values of Christianity and transplanted them to the earthly and linear time of history. Christian eternity became the future of liberal evolutionism.

Here is the final contradiction, and all the divergences and differences I have mentioned culminate in it. A society is essentially defined by its position as regards time. The United States, because of its origin and its intellectual and political history, is a society oriented toward the future. The extraordinary spatial mobility of America, a nation constantly on the move, has often been pointed out. In the realm of beliefs and mental attitudes, mobility in time corresponds to physical and geographical displacement. The American lives on the very edge of the now, always ready to leap toward the future. The country's foundations are in the future, not in the past, Or, rather, its past, the act of its founding, was a promise of the future, and each time the United States returns to its source, to its past, it rediscovers the future.

Mexico's orientation, as has been seen, was just the opposite. First came the rejection of criticism, and with it rejection of the notion of change: its ideal is to conserve the image of divine immutability. Second, it has a plurality of pasts, all present and at war within every Mexican's soul. Cortés and Montezuma are still alive in Mexico. At the time of that great crisis the Mexican Revolution, the most radical faction, that of Zapata and his peasants, proposed not new forms of social organization but a return to communal ownership of land. The rebelling peasants were asking for the devolution of the land; that is, they wanted to go back to a pre-Columbian form of ownership which had been respected by the Spaniards. The image the revolutionaries instinctively made for themselves of a Golden Age lay in the remotest past. Utopia for them was not the construction of a future but a return to the source, to the beginning. The traditional Mexican attitude toward time has been expressed in this way by a Mexican poet, Ramon López Velarde: "Motherland, be still the same, faithful to each day's mirror."

In the seventeenth century, Mexican society was richer and more prosperous than American society. This situation lasted until the first half on the eighteenth century. To prove that it was so, one need only glance at the cities of those days, with their monuments and buildings — Mexico City and Boston, Puebla and Philadelphia. Then everything changed. In 1847, the United States invaded Mexico, occupied it, and imposed on it terrible and heavy conditions of peace. A century later, the United States became the dominant world power. An unusual conjunction of circumstances of a material, technological, political, ideological, and human order explains the prodigious development of the United States. But in the small religious communities of seventeenth-century New England, the future was already in bud: political democracy, capitalism, and social and economic development. In Mexico, something very different has occurred. At the end of the eighteenth century, the Mexican ruling classes — especially the intellectuals — discovered that the principles that had founded their society condemned it to immobility and backwardness. They undertook a twofold revolution: separation from Spain and modernization of the country through the adoption of new republican and democratic principles. Their examples were the American Revolution and the French Revolution. They gained independence from Spain, but the adoption of new principles was not enough: Mexico changed its laws, not its social, economic, and cultural realities.

During much of the nineteenth century, Mexico suffered an endemic civil war and three invasions by foreign powers — the United States, Spain, and France. In the latter part of the century, order was reestablished, but at the expense of democracy. In the name of liberal ideology and the positivism of Comte and Spencer, a military dictatorship was imposed which lasted more than thirty years. It was a period of peace and appreciable material development — also of increasing penetration by foreign capital, especially from England and the United States. The Mexican Revolution of 1910 set itself to change direction. It succeeded only in part: Mexican democracy is not yet a reality, and the great advances achieved in certain quarters have been nullified or are in danger because of excessive political centralization, excessive population growth, social inequality, the collapse of higher education, and the actions of the economic monopolies, among them those from the United States. Like all the other states of this century, the Mexican state has had an enormous, monstrous development. A curious contradiction: The state has been the agent of modernization, but it has been unable to modernize itself entirely. It is a hybrid of the Spanish patrimonialist state of the seventeenth century and the modern bureaucracies of the West. As for its relationship with the United States, that is still the old relationship of strong and weak, oscillating between indifference and abuse, deceit and cynicism. Most Mexicans hold the justifiable conviction that the treatment received by their country is unfair.

Above and beyond success and failure, Mexico is still asking itself the question that has occurred to most clear-thinking Mexicans since the end of the eighteenth century: the question about modernization. In the nineteenth century, it was believed that to adopt the new democratic and liberal principles was enough. Today, after almost two centuries of setbacks, we have realized that countries change very slowly, and that if such changes are to be fruitful they must be in harmony with the past and the traditions of each nation. And so Mexico has to find its own road to modernity. Our past must not be an obstacle but a starting point. This is extremely difficult, given the nature of our traditions — difficult but not impossible. To avoid new disasters, we Mexicans must reconcile ourselves with our past: only in this way shall we succeed in finding a route to modernity.

The ideological wars of the twentieth century are no less ferocious than the wars of religion of the seventeenth century. When I was young, the idea that we were witnessing the final crisis of capitalism was fashionable among intellectuals. Now we understand that the crisis is not of a socioeconomic system but of our whole civilization. It is a general worldwide crisis, and its most extreme, acute, and dangerous expression is found in the situation of the Soviet Union and its satellites. The contradictions of totalitarian "socialism" are more profound and irreconcilable than those of the capitalist democracies.

The sickness of the West is moral rather than social and economic. It is true that the economic problems are serious and that they have not been solved. Poverty has not disappeared, despite affluence. Several groups — women and racial, religious, and linguistic minorities — still are or feel excluded. But the real, most profound discord lies in the soul. The future has become the realm of horror, and the present has turned into a desert. The liberal societies spin tirelessly, not forward but round and round. If they change, they are not transfigured. The hedonism of the West is the other face of desperation; its skepticism is not wisdom but renunciation; its nihilism ends in suicide and in inferior forms of credulity, such as political fanaticisms and magical chimeras. The empty place left by Christianity in the modern soul is filled not by philosophy but by the crudest superstitions. Our eroticism is a technique, not an art or a passion.

I will not continue. The evils of the West have been described often enough, most recently by Solzhenitsyn, a man of admirable character. However, although his description seems to me accurate, his judgement of the causes of the sickness does not, nor does the remedy he proposes. We cannot renounce the critical tradition of the West; nor can we return to the medieval theocratic state. Dungeons of the Inquisition are not an answer to the Gulag camps. It is not worthwhile substituting the church-state for the party-state, one orthodoxy for another. The only effective arm against orthodoxies is criticism, and in order to defend ourselves against the vices of intolerance and fanaticism our only recourse is the exercise of the opposing virtues: tolerance and freedom of spirit. I do not disown Montesquieu, Hume, Kant....

Chapter 11

Cultural Integration in Latin America at the Millennium

Carlos Monsiváis

Who or what is involved in cultural integration? Does it imply an integration among the countries of Latin America, or an integration between Latin America and the international community, or between Latin America and the cultural industry of the United States? Is it a process of flow or a kind of "Free Culture Agreement"? Since the 1970s, several factors constitute interventions in the cultural field — the repeated and deep-rooted economic crises, the burden of authoritarian regimes, the inefficiencies and the grave difficulties which arise within democratically inclined governments — all within the panorama of advances and fallbacks that do nothing to lighten the summit meetings nor the manifestos of good will. Therefore, it is well worth examining some common elements:

- The emergence of mid-to-large cities, eager to resemble the United States, with chain restaurants and the cult of the automobile. This often depressing uniformity is not helped by the meager results of a postmodern architecture.

- The phenomena of post-secularization, including the demographic explosion of beliefs and esoteric convictions.

- An increased tolerance that breaks the hegemony of traditionalism.

- Democracy achieved "from the bottom up" (for the moment, the only conceivable kind), with its inevitable repercussions: the cult of civil society and the lack of trust in all political parties.

- An immense distrust of utopian thinking, one of the consequences of the collapse of socialism. Add to this the crisis of the left whose renovating impulse is curbed by the weakness of its platform. Also, Marxism, once so important to university education, has vanished publicly, replaced by diverse theories and theoreticians, from Norberto Bobbio and John Rawls to Isaiah Berlin.

Translated by Roberto Tejada.

- The clustering (of course, more psychological than theoretical) of the various democratic "progressive" sectors, as we used to say, in the face of a commanding neoliberalism and the pseudo-religion of the free market (rampant capitalism as a moral obligation).

- The crisis of the publishing business has made the Spanish industry the major bibliographic nexus for Latin America. The number of copies per edition has been reduced; poetry hardly sells, and the systems of distribution are inefficient. Excluding the promotional apparatus of the large Spanish publishing houses, authors are only known in their respective countries or, more often than not, in their respective cities. Circulation with regard to cultural magazines has become strictly national or regional.

- We witness the massive movement toward a predominantly visual culture that minimizes the achievements and perspectives of traditional humanistic culture which once belonged to the minority that created national projects.

- An ecological conscience, though still diffuse, has been activated in urban and rural landscapes where industrial devastation, pollution, deforestation, and the thermal-inversion effect reign.

- The growing impact of the cultural industry produced by the United States. As for feature films or video rentals in Latin America, more than 80 percent are North American. As for compact-disk sales, nearly 50 percent are represented by North American rock music. Best-sellers from the United States prevail, from Tom Clancy to the most recent self-help publication. The exceptions can be counted: *Like Water for Chocolate* by Laura Esquivel and *House of the Spirits* by Isabel Allende. As before, there are strong links to the different centers of power: Spain, the publishing metropolis; New York, the metropolis of artistic legitimation; Paris, the metropolis of intellectual vogues.

- Feminism, or the array of theories and practices which aim to increase women's rights, has had many important repercussions in the field of culture. Among these is the promotion of literature written by women.

- Universities are rapidly developing, and the rate of students and teachers is extraordinarily high if compared to the past. Postgraduate work, preferably in the United States, begins to render the undergraduate degree a mere high school diploma. In the 1980s, however, the faith in a university degree deteriorated as the unemployment rate rose in the ranks of college graduates, especially those from public universities.

What do we know of the cultural environment of Latin America in situations over-determined by an economy which never manages to take off at all and by a politics which never gains the required credibility? Is the imposing globalization compatible with the new isolationism? Does it make sense to speak of a "globalization of the periphery"? Television is the great supplier of information, in areas where the commercial apparatus submerges, obscures, and diminishes local and national efforts. The exchange of cultural incentives is mechanically added to the substitution of imported goods. In the meanwhile, we are showered by apocalyptic warnings as to the loss of identity which, ultimately, is never lost.

There is still an element that needs to be underlined, one that has been present throughout the century but became decisive in the 1960s: Americanization. I do not mean the measurable benefits of an international culture, a legitimate and inevitable matter, but rather the series of factors that reinforce dependence:

- The meaning of what is contemporary is decided in the United States, regarding definitions of modernity and fashions of all kinds, including intellectual vogues.

- Among the middle classes and the bourgeoisie, the American way of life is compulsively imitated. This, reinforced daily via television, transforms certain North American cities (Miami, Houston, Dallas, Los Angeles, New York) into Meccas or "ceremonial centers" for Latin Americans of varying social classes.

- Youth culture almost entirely depends on what is promoted in North America: from rock groups or fusion bands to clothing, the use of earrings by men, and so forth.

- Television, specifically via cable TV and the parabolic antenna, makes information with regard to North America a specific knowledge for Latin Americans.

- The relationship established between society and information is increasingly regulated by the North American model of the news format.

When Civilization and Barbarity Were Quite Distinct

How did this process come about? Throughout the nineteenth century, the countries of Ibero-America were united by the burden and sense of history, the other name given to the fortuitous construction of stability, which involved educational and cultural development, constitutions, civil and penal codes, communications, liberal and conservative exasperation with the burden of the indigenous, the myth-making of *mestizaje* (or miscegenation), the buttressing of racial prejudice, the rhythm of migrations, as well as the fragile balance between what it means to want and what it means to have. And history, often synonymous with destiny, has at its disposal a legacy of emblems of cohesion and identity: heroes who serve as libertarian messengers, as players in a version of the trial of Christ, or as a messianic hope. In the repertoire of paladins, a common culture is founded: Bolívar, San Martín, Hidalgo, Morelos, Mina, Artigas, Caupolicán, O'Higgins, Juárez, Martí, Céspedes. These figures, with their efforts and, almost perforce, by their martyrdom, psychologically and culturally create a unique category: the ideal of the inhabitant of an independent country, who is no longer subject to any monarchy, though he is still far from exercising his rights. Also, each hero, through his defeats and frustrations, in his own way details the difficulties as to the integration of nations. (Very few are the emblem, like Benito Juárez, of irrefutable victories.)

At the beginning of the twentieth century, illiteracy predominated in Latin America. The insistent attention focused on increasing literacy was a consequence of the generosity shown by liberals and revolutionaries and also of the project of industrialization which required of workers much more accuracy. Thanks to that emphasis, for several years teaching was allotted a privileged place (two obvious examples: José Vasconcelos in Mexico and Gabriela Mistral in Chile). There was a unanimous response to Sarmiento's formula "Civilization or Barbarity": Civilization was the only answer, and civilization is the sum total of books, symphonies, illustrious figures, masterpieces of the theater, a revindication of the indigenous past, and so forth. Barbarity is underdevelopment, illiteracy, and ignorance as to the superior value of Western culture. This situation existed despite the subjugation on the part of governments who used a strong arm and despite the extremely scarce value attributed to democracy.

In the first half of the twentieth century, to speak of culture in Latin America was to affirm the corpus of Western civilization in addition to national and Latin American contributions. Despite the prevailing intellectualism, the devotion to knowledge was widespread, and the motto of Mexico's National Autonomous University, "The spirit speaks through my race," coined by Vasconcelos, demanded the following translation: The only ones authorized to speak in the name of the race (the masses) were those in whom the spirit resided — university graduates, the enlightened class. Guided by this faith in the powers of a select minority, intellectuals and artists produced notable works, and they created, championed, and investigated. Particularly outstanding in the cultural mythology are the names of the magazines where the groups and personalities published: *Sur* (Argentina), *Orígenes* (Cuba), *Contemporáneos* (Mexico), and *Asomante* (Puerto Rico).

The Holy Grail of Modernity

By the 1960s, modernity was everything, and, most importantly, it was the proximity with the time of the metropolis, the severed circle of underdevelopment as stated by Alfonso Reyes in his phrase: "We have arrived late to the banquet of Western civilization." Throughout a brief period, the idea of revolution became identified with extreme modernity, which is why Cuba's Casa de las Américas began vigorously to promote the Latin American novel.

Inevitably, the rise in secondary and higher education transformed the university into the natural place of resistance during the apogee of Latin American dictatorships. Culture ceased to be that which separated a select minority from the masses, and it became, in theory, the right of all. And the cultural marginality of Latin America was entirely rejected, or at least the eternal nature of that condition was disputed. A very active minority reevaluated the contributions of the past and present and avowed, with an openly international attitude, that it was possible to be up-to-date. The feelings of inferiority with regard to the centers of knowledge were eradicated or at least considerably reduced. This did not automatically provide libraries, nor did it lend an infrastructure to scientific research. It did, however, put an end to the feelings of isolationism. Also, the panorama was modified, with varying results, by the rise of a huge industry of culture and the media. On the positive side, an enormous sector, which lacked even the most minimal information, began to enjoy the classics of literature: Bach, Beethoven, and Mozart; as well as exhibitions of Picasso and Diego Rivera. Reading, in general, increased; classical music was promoted, and classical and contemporary art began to be appreciated by a wider audience. There were now vast sectors which, in their own way, enjoyed the masterpieces of Western culture and, increasingly often, products from other cultures as well.

Everything Bores Me Except What's Usually Considered Entertaining

In trying to establish the cultural communication, or integration, of Latin America, dictatorships of taste interpose. Among them, most notoriously, are those which maintain a hegemony over daily life. Whether it be in Mexico, Venezuela, Costa Rica, Bolivia, or Colombia, for forty years a single model has established the norms. With a clamor, this model determines what is *boring* and what is *entertaining*. It is a model followed both by public officials and humorless critics and is the very project and mold of the new identity. Several factors are at the root of this: the "take-what-you-get" disdain of the public which gratefully laughs at awful jokes, while suffering through the absurdities of elemental dramas that occasionally remind them of their human nature. And many who criticize "just for the sake of it" consider themselves immune: they are different; they are not fooled by television, which they watch only a few hours a day and from which they extract most of their information about society.

Latin America has paid most dearly for this singular version of boredom and entertainment as television moves into daily life, culture into politics. The collective identity, always shifting for reasons of creativity and preservation, has been paralyzed in its prejudices. To entertain, in this authoritarian landscape, is to make time pass so that it might not occur to anyone that such time might be spent more beneficially, for the seal of productivity is deposited in industry and technology. Free time is a parenthesis between one serious activity (economically productive) and the next, and tedium is simply the worst threat. If you are bored, you will be left without your favorite identity, the identity of having take-what-you-get fun.

Much more than a "cultural penetration" by North American imperialism (a term that supposes a spiritually virgin Latin America submerged in its ancestral values, vestal virgin of traditions which alone succeed in banishing the enemy), I am referring to the prevalent notions of entertainment and tedium. That is what demonstrates the subjection to Americanization, that great commercial and ideological project. The Latin American public is enthusiastic about the "free time" spent in the American way, though compromises are inherent in the leap from a former identity to a superficial integration.

What is entertaining? What is boring? If these questions were put to vital and secondary issues, we would arrive, I believe, at a more accurate image of television and of the individual. Do the following stimulate or bore us to tears: intellectual matters, national values, ethical issues, and provincial life, or "variety" shows from the Rio Grande to Patagonia, the interviews with singers who cannot sing, and musical groups that entrust themselves to lip-sync? Is there any middle ground? Is it true that television viewers can be divided by age and that each age has a unique temperament? Is involuntary humor the only known defense against these televised ordeals? Is commercial television the formal depository of moral values? Do the televised church services from the Basilica of Guadalupe renew our Mexican identity, or do they simply integrate the credo with satellite dishes? Behind the myth in which the fastidious is boring and the entertaining is fun lies the debate with regard to exercising pluralism, a crucial point for Latin America at this end of the century. Opposed to this are the monopolies of political, economic, religious, and, to some degree, cultural power. And by explicitly denying diversity, and by only accepting it via advertising, television reaffirms its disdain for pluralism and praises monolithic identity and the integration it excludes.

It was comfort and complicity that permitted a select few to impose a taste in the field of leisure time, and after four decades most people adhere to that imposition. In order to break free of it, and to give way to a genuine diversity regarding taste and criteria, the first thing we must do is to demobilize censorship, perhaps the most effective instrument in limiting the mental horizon of the public (as such). With the censorship we experience, it is difficult (if not impossible) to forge television programming that is contemporary, that permits viewers to renovate the criteria regarding entertainment and boredom. If we fail to eliminate censorship and the facile attitude toward the public, television in Latin America will continue to nourish the modernization that fails to modernize, among traditions that begin to crumble.

"To Be Modern Is Not to Worry About the Pre-Moderns"

Today, millions of Latin Americans want to counteract the monotony and circularity of their lives. They want to have fun; they want to be entertained and to think in novel ways. Certainly the opportunities are different, but inertia and the lack of a social or government project predominate. Few people continue reading after finishing their studies; few are allowed to change their cultural habits. The majority, in large cities or small towns, would find no books to purchase anyway.

Equally devastating is the lack of information. The process of cultural information has become increasingly emphasized, and we all live under the miserable definitions of "modernization." According to the prevailing criteria, "to be modernized" simply means eliminating "inefficiency," to make (very sectarian) technological advances the only sign of existence, to imitate the way in which North American society assimilates technology, and to privatize the economy to the maximum. In the arrangement of hierarchies for the nation, culture has no place whatsoever.

Can an exterior modernization occur following the orders from above? Who, in the final instance, pays the high cost of modernization, and how many millions are consigned to oblivion "because there is no other solution"? The scenario of a fast-track modernization is a dramatic one. For example, what will happen to 300 million Latin Americans once their purchasing power has been minimally resolved? How will they begin to take an interest in the ballet or the opera? How will they accept the simultaneity of taste: classical music, rock, boleros, Asian music, salsa music, African music? How will they walk into a bookstore without feeling intimidated? How will they know what magazines they should be reading and what plays they should attend? How will they develop a literacy in film? People fail to go to the theater because they have never actually attended before. People do not read, or do so almost symbolically, because it is a difficult activity, and they never acquired the habit during childhood. With regard to the arts, the working class is usually apathetic. "If I am never informed, how can I be motivated?" Official culture does not believe in campaigns to inform or to form taste. Instead, it is involved in the restricted offers accompanying a publication which are likely to be more expensive than the publication itself. The underprivileged are offered the writing on the wall: If you don't read the classics, if you're not passionate about the fauves and the expressionists, if you can't recognize the difference between the pre-Rafaelites and the baroque masters, if you're not aware of each new publication, it's your fault, the result of your negligence, your love of hoarding, your mental incapacity, your natural indifference toward the works of the spirit.

Now, underdeveloped or Third World countries are defined by the lack of cultural support. Without proper libraries and bookstores, with the worst conceivable programming in film and video, with book sales at a minimum and museums empty, without budgeting for theater and dance, without access to newspapers and quality magazines (for someone who earns minimum wage, to read a daily paper would mean spending 15 percent of his monthly income), subject to brutal doses of television glitter, immersed in a functional illiteracy, millions of Latin Americans identify the lack of cultural rights with the absence of civil rights, and this generalization includes small towns, the urban margins, and mid-sized cities, and it implies the large cities, for therein lies a relative abundance of possibilities.

The Foreseeable Future

Because they are useless, predictions tend to be hopeless, but we can begin to see a trend in what is considered cultural life in Latin America: the development and logical continuity of present-day tendencies. Functional illiteracy will expand, and reading will be relegated to a secondary status, with the consent of both the government and society. "Gutenberg's Galaxy" will be perpetuated, though reduced, and television more than ever will be the great vehicle for internal communication among societies. Newspapers and magazines, as in the nineteenth century, will concentrate the work of writers, for most of them will be convinced of the limitations of the book and its readership. The criteria of modernism (and post-modernism) will be decisive, and the aim will be to update societies by enthroning the formula of the "New Man," no longer a revolutionary but an agent of "Total Quality" — technologized, super-informed, well-communicated, efficient, and productive. It is he who will replace the "typical" Latin American — idle, pre-technological, unreliable, lacking incentives, prone to absenteeism, and inept. This cultural and work-related demand of the "New Man," of an out-and-out "mental modernization," will devolve on a public which is the victim of an indiscriminate modernization, a public that is deterministically convinced of its conditions of poverty. Here the responses must vary, but surely migrations will intensify; the deterioration or disorganization of the traditional groupings (family, social class, ethnicity) will continue; the standstill in the majority's income and in their standard of life will become more accentuated, and regional conflicts will begin to multiply, though perhaps not with the spectacularity of the Zapatista Army of National Liberation in Chiapas, with its classic blend of daring and despair. In short, social frustration will increasingly outweigh economic growth.

Under such a dark panorama, the achievements of culture are invigorated; it is, perhaps, the only available instrument of social mobility for the majority. It is the great humanist element of balance during a moment of crisis. It is the natural arena for reflection and the site where societies mature. If that is not all, it is at least a considerable advantage.

Chapter 12

Cultural Transmission and the American Cosmos

Orlando Patterson

The modern process of global cultural interaction has repeatedly been subjected to two criticisms. The first is that it threatens the diversity and particularism of the world's cultures, resulting in a deadening homogenization of the human cultural experience. The other is that this growing global uniformity results from the dominance of America's culture — that, in effect, global culture is nothing more than American cultural imperialism. Hannah Arendt's lament that we have been brought to a "global present without a common past [which] threatens to render all traditions and all particular past histories irrelevant" is typical of the first. Theodor Adorno's famous diatribe against American popular music is the *locus classicus* of the second. Both objections are without foundation.

The argument that Americanization is resulting in the homogenization of the world ignores the increased vitality of local cultures and ethnicities in recent times and the complexity of global cultural diffusion, in particular the extent to which so-called peripheral regions are increasingly contributing to American popular culture and to the world music scene. Nor does it explain the emergence of a special kind of regional system, what I shall call the regional cosmos, or the great cultural divisions in America itself. The American cosmos, as we shall see, is not a single cultural space, but is divided among three Americas: traditional America, multicultural America, and ecumenical America.

The Diffusion of Global Culture

Industrialization and modernization both entailed the spread of common sets of behaviors and attitudes within the context of economic change. However, the globalization of culture is also independent of whatever economic changes are occurring in a particular region or society. Traditionally, the transmission of culture across societies was facilitated by two main

This article originally appeared as *Global Culture and the American Cosmos* and is reprinted with permission from the Andy Warhol Foundation for the Visual Arts, from the Foundation's Paper Series on the Arts, Culture, and Society.

media: migration and literacy. People learned about other cultures either through traveling themselves or from travelers, or by reading about other cultures and adopting or adapting what they learned. These traditional media could, under certain circumstances, be effective means for the transmission of cultures across the globe.

The distinctive feature of literary transmissions, and all diffusions through individuals except during mass migrations, is that they tend to be largely confined to elites, or, where not, to enclaves of non-elite persons cut off from the mass of their societies. This was true of the diffusion of Hellenism in the Mediterranean world and was largely true of the imperial influence on the societies of Asia and Africa. Until the end of the Second World War, Westernism was largely confined to a tiny minority of the populations of these continents, largely the educated native elites and urban workers. Since the 1950s, however, this has changed radically. The globalization of culture, largely (although by no means solely, as the spread of Islam indicates) through the impact of, and *reaction to*, the diffusion of Western popular and elite culture, has not only greatly increased in terms of its spread over the surface of the world, but in terms of the depth to which it has influenced the populations of other societies.

Four factors account for this sudden change of pace. The first is the spread of mass literacy throughout the world, which resulted from the new nations of the postcolonial era investing vast sums and human energy in their educational systems, the structure and content of which were largely influenced by Western models. The second is the rise of mass communication. The third is the growth of global organizations, both private and public, such as the multinational corporation, the United Nations, the World Bank, the IMF, and the large number of regional agencies, themselves often modeled on and directly influenced and promoted by the former. The fourth is the revolution in long-distance transportation, which has resulted in the emergence of an entirely new kind of global, or more properly, subglobal system, the regional cosmos. The most remarkable of these emerging regional cosmoses is the West Atlantic system, encompassed by the eastern seaboard of North America and the circum-Caribbean societies of Central America and the islands.

The Global Popular Music Culture

The emergence of the regional cosmoses provides perhaps the best evidence of the complexity of global cultural diffusion. But before turning to the subject of their development, let us consider one example of global cultural diffusion — namely, how mass communication has facilitated the diffusion and creation of global popular musical culture. I choose to focus on popular music because it is in this area of the globalization process that the strongest claims of homogenization have been made. Its classic statement was given by the musicologist Alan Lomax who, in 1968, lamented the presumed passing of the great local cultures of the world under the impact of American popular culture, which, he feared, would lead to global rootlessness and alienation as the peoples of the earth all sank into the desolate gloom of the great, global "cultural grey-out."[1]

As someone who has studied this process in a Third World society that has perhaps been more exposed to the full glare of American culture than nearly any other — namely, Jamaica — I can say unequivocally that such charges are utter nonsense. It is simply not true that the diffusion of Western culture, especially at the popular level, leads to the homogenization of the culture of the world. Indeed, my research, and that of the best scholars working in this area, suggests that just the opposite is the case. Western-American cultural influence has generated enormous cultural production, in some cases amounting to near hypercreativity in the popular cultures of the world.

If what I say is correct, it must be wondered where the popular misconception of the homogenizing effect of the Western impact came from. One source is the propagandistic reaction of traditional cultural gatekeepers in Third World societies whose monopoly and influence has been threatened by the Western cultural impact. That impact, in generating new cultural forms, invariably stimulates the emergence of new and competing cultural agents and managers. To monopolize the cultural resources of a country is to exercise enormous power, not to mention to control economic resources. What usually upsets traditional cultural gatekeepers about the Western impact on their mass cultures is less the content of Western culture — because this is invariably transformed — and more the choice it immediately offers to the consumers of culture.

The second source of misconceptions about the impact of Westernism comes from important segments of the cultural gatekeepers in the West itself, on both the right and the left, who think and talk about this issue. The more abstract of these complaints about the influence of American global popular culture stem from elitist, postmodernist pessimism of the sort that stimulates similar complaints about the stultifying effects of popular culture on the working class of the West. Cultural critic Paul Willis has recently taken issue with these pretentious criticisms. He notes that people never simply absorb cultural messages passively. There is always what Willis calls symbolic work at play: "The incandescence is not simply a surface market quality. It produces, is driven by, and reproduces further forms and varieties for everyday symbolic work and creativity, some of which remain in the everyday and in common culture far longer than they do on the market."[2]

There is a great deal of sloppy and ill-informed criticism of American-ization in what passes for serious, empirically based research. It is simply assumed that illiterate and semiliterate Third World peoples are powerless in their responses to Western popular culture. Experts on the subject have in mind a world of passive consumers, homogenized and manipulated into Marx's notorious sack of (Westernized) potatoes.[3] It is nothing of the sort. The semi- and non-literate masses of the Third World invariably react to Western cultural influence in a nonpassive manner, reinterpreting what they receive in the light of their own cultures and experience. One of my favorite examples of this is the story about the British officer in a remote part of northern Greece following the general elections in Britain at the end of the Second World War. The officer asked a Greek peasant if he knew the results of the elections. "Oh yes," replied the peasant excitedly, "the Labour party has won the elections, the king has been assassinated, and Mr. Churchill and his party have fled to the mountains!"

Either the Western cultural form is reinterpreted in light of traditional meanings, or Western meanings are adapted to traditional patterns. In any case, something new, although still local, emerges. As the musicologist Peter Manuel points out, not only do local cultures "adapt foreign elements in distinctly idiosyncratic ways that substantially alter their function, context, and meaning," but even what appears to Western ears and perception to be a major intrusion, may, in fact, be so shallow functionally to the native listener as to not even be perceived. This is true, for example, of the influence of American music on the thriving Indian pop culture.[4]

In their comparative analysis of eight cultures, musicologists Deanna Robinson, Elizabeth Buck, and others have demonstrated — in my opinion, conclusively — that "world musical homogenization is not occurring." As they put it, "even though information-age economic forces are building an international consumership for centrally produced and distributed popular music, other factors are pulling in the opposite direction. They are encouraging not only what we call 'indigenization' of popular music forms and production but also new, eclectic combinations of world musical elements, combinations that contradict the continuing constraints of national boundaries and global capitalism."[5]

Furthermore, the common notion that the globalization of culture, especially on the popular level, is a one-way process, from the Western metropolis to the passive and vulnerable periphery, is simply not the case, although it is certainly true that the major diffusionary source of this culture is a single Western country: the United States.

Not homogenization, then, but the revitalization and generation of new musical forms have been the effects of the global exchange process. Some of these forms remain local, providing greater choice and stimulus to the local culture. Examples of such revitalization include the modernization of the traditional Camerounian *makassi* style with the introduction of the acoustic rhythm guitar; the development of the *highlife* music of Ghana, which fused traditional forms with jazz, rock, and Trinidadian calypso rhythms; the vibrant local modernization of traditional Afro-Arab music in Kenya. Elsewhere, musical forms under Western impact have broken out of their provincial boundaries to become regional currency, as, for example, the Trinidadian and American pop influenced *kru-krio* music of Sierra Leone, which swept West Africa and beyond during the 1960s and 1970s; the Brazilian *sambo*, the pan-American *salsa; merengue* (the latter of Dominican Republic origin); the originally Cuban *nueva trova*, which became a radical pan-Latin form, stimulating the even more radical and pan-Latin *nueva cancion*; and the Colombian *cumbia*, which has become an important part of the music of the Tex-Mex regional cosmos. And there are those musical forms that experience their fifteen minutes of fame as the latest fad in the "world music" scene: the Argentinean *tango;* the Algerian *rai*; the Zairian *soukous*; the Brazilian *bossa nova*.

Out of Jamaica

One of the most globally successful cultural creations of a Third World people is the musical form known as *reggae*. Indeed, the development of reggae perhaps more than any other musical form illustrates the complexity of global cultural interaction. The creation of the Jamaican working classes and lumpen proletariat, reggae emerged in the late 1950s from a variety of influences, especially American. Jamaica had always had a rich musical tradition, originating mainly in the music of West Africa brought over by the slaves, but also influenced in its lyrical and melodic lines by British, especially Celtic, popular music of the late eighteenth and nineteenth centuries. At the turn of the century, a popular secular form, *mento*, ideal for dancing, emerged. Similar to the Trinidad calypso in its topical and satirical lyrics and in its reliance on the guitar for a Latinate ostinato, *mento* soon established itself as *the* traditional popular music of the island.

By the late 1950s, however, young working-class Jamaicans had grown weary of *mento*. What they did like were the rhythm-and-blues records being brought back by farm laborers returning from cutting cane in Florida and the "cowboy music" or bluegrass they picked up on short-wave early in the mornings. Aspiring young Jamaican singers — including the teenage Bob Marley, Peter Tosh, Bob Andy, and numerous others — began singing imitations of American soul songs at the many talent parades that preceded the weekend triple bills at the working-class cinemas. These imitations were, at first, ghastly renditions of the original. (I can still recall hearing a pimpled, short-haired Bob Marley singing an American soul song hopelessly out of tune.) At this point, Jamaica would seem to have had the worst of all possible worlds. A delightful native musical tradition had been abandoned, and in its place the island found its middle class swooning over syrupy white American ballads while its lower class sang imitations of African American music.

What happened next, however, demonstrates just how complex the dialectics between local and foreign influences that generate the global culture are. First of all, the imitations were so bad that they were unwittingly original. Furthermore, the Jamaicans instinctively brought their own local musical cadences and rhythms to bear on the tunes being imitated. This coincided with an infusion of the very African music of the Afro-Jamaican cults, which was lifted straight from the "laboring" movements made by cult celebrants as they worked themselves up to the point of spirit possession. Both the movement and the accompanying rhythm were secularized (in a manner similar to the crossover from gospel to soul music among African Americans), and a wholly new musical form and accompanying dance, known as *ska*, was created.

At the time — the late 1950s and early 1960s — the vast majority of working-class Jamaicans were still too poor to buy record players or expensive imported records. This led to the formation of the *sound system*, a hi-fidelity system outfitted with enormous bass speakers, which the owners rented out, along with their record collections and themselves in the role of disc jockey. The disc jockeys, partly out of boredom, partly out of increasing dissatisfaction with the rhythmic patterns of the imported African American records, but above all, out of a desire to give a "live" quality to the performance of their systems, started to deliberately play around with the records as they were being played. They voiced over the imported records with their own rhythmic commentary, improving their "riddim" as they understood it, either through grunts and screams, or through an accompanying screed that sometimes made sense or was sometimes mere nonsense lyrics, which mattered little since the voice was actually being used as an additional bass instrument. This was rapidly to become a distinctive feature of reggae. The disc jockey would also "play" the turntable, stopping and pushing the record as it turned on the platter in order to induce strange new sounds. This, too, was later to become an essential part of the music, except that the strange noises were to be made through the manipulation of sophisticated studio electronics.

What emerged from these activities was another distinctive musical form, *dub*. When the disc jockeys were unable to match the love lyrics of the imported black American rhythm-and-blues songs, they resorted to what they knew best, local politics. Thus was born reggae *dub*, with its strong emphasis on the political, a clear departure from popular American music, black or white.

At about the same time that these developments were taking place, the Ras Tafari cult, a millenarian back-to-Africa movement that was the religious component of the reaction to Western influence, was taking hold among the Jamaican proletariat of the Kingston shanties. The spiritualism and radical racial ideology of the cult — a religious form of negritude, exemplifying Sartre's "anti-racist racism" — greatly appealed to the very people developing the music, and it was not long before the two merged, Rastafarian theology giving substance and ideological content to what were previously soppy imported lyrics or garbled political chatter.

The music swiftly went through several formal changes, first from ska to *rock steady*, a more complex slow-tempo music, and finally, in response to the demands of the entrepreneurs who ran the weekend dance halls and who wanted music with a faster beat so their patrons would drink more of the Red Stripe beer on which they largely depended for their profits, to reggae.

Reggae swiftly caught on, not only among locals, but also the American tourists who were now visiting Jamaica in increasing numbers. Several major singers emerged in the late 1960s and early 1970s, the most successful of whom was Bob Marley, whose enormous showmanship and song-writing ability were important in internationalizing the music. However, one other factor was equally important in explaining the rapid spread of reggae and its eventual emergence as a global musical form. This was the mass movements of Jamaican working-class migrants. The first such movement was to Britain, where Jamaicans effectively transformed what was a previously all-white country into a multiracial society. By 1964, a thinly Anglicized version of ska known as *blue beat* was already in vogue.[6] Today, reggae has been completely embraced by white British youth, who now view it as an integral part of their culture.[7] From its British base, it was to spread rapidly throughout continental Europe and north and sub-Saharan Africa.

Similarly, reggae spread to the United States as a result of a second mass migration of the Jamaican working class, which began with the liberalization of American immigration laws in the early 1960s. A new kind of West Indian migrant now entered America, not the relatively well-educated, highly motivated petty-bourgeois migrants of previous generations, but the working-class and lumpen-proletarian people from the Kingston slums. Eventually, the reggae music these new migrants brought over with them, along with their disk jockeys and dance halls (as well as their gangs, the notorious posses), were to influence black American youth, but what is interesting is how long it took to do so. Black Americans, in fact, strongly resisted most versions of reggae. Reggae, however, rapidly caught on among the white college students of America, especially after the enormous success of the reggae movie, *The Harder They Come*, and soon broke out of the campus circuit with the success of Bob Marley and other international stars, such as Jimmy Cliff and Peter Tosh.[8]

Eventually, by the late 1970s and early 1980s, even the underclass African American young began to respond to reggae. They were simply unable to prevent themselves from listening to the version of reggae brought over to the ghettoes by the latest wave of underclass Kingston migrants: the dance-hall music. The fact that they also soon developed a healthy respect for the violent Jamaican posses also explains their changed attitude.

The music had gone full circle, from its beginnings in the crude imitations of 1950s' African American lower-class music, to the late 1970s' and early 1980s' imitations of dance-hall dub by the New York underclass. The American music that emerged from this extraordinary proletarian cross-fertilization was *rap*, the first popular American music to have an explicitly political lyrical content. The Jamaicans had repaid their debt.

The West Atlantic Regional Cosmos

The transmission of reggae to the American center from the Jamaican periphery not only illustrates the complexity of global cultural interaction but was also a forerunner of a much more complex process that has now integrated parts of the United States with other countries as deeply or more deeply than those parts are integrated with other regions of America. This aspect of the globalization of culture, which has resulted in the development of regional cosmoses, is entirely new. Indeed, it has emerged only over the past two decades or so, largely because it was dependent upon the revolution in cheap mass transportation.

The regional cosmos is best conceived of as a system of flows between a metropolitan center and a set of politically independent satellite countries within what the urban sociologist Saskia Sassen calls a "transnational space."[9] People, wealth, ideas, and cultural patterns move in both directions, influencing both the metropolitan center and the peripheral areas, although asymmetrically. Although they are similar in many respects to other migratory systems, such as those of the Mediterranean, there are several unique features of the regional cosmoses that are of special importance to the problem of the globalization of culture.

In the West Atlantic regional cosmos, made up of eastern America and the circum-Caribbean societies, the peripheral areas are either contiguous with or within easy reach of the dominant metropolitan society.[10] The separate units are legally autonomous, but sovereignty becomes merely a resource to be used in the interaction between the main collective actors. In spite of legal restrictions on the movement of peoples, there is a vast flow in both directions — legal and illegal migrants from the periphery, tourists and investors from the center. There is no simple flow of cheap labor to capital in this system, as in the classic colonial regimes. Skilled and cheap labor flow in both directions. Legal and illegal capital also move in both directions.

The Third World countries of the periphery are only too eager to attract such capital, but with capitalization their economies become dualized, as is true of the center, between an urban-modern sector and a traditional-rural one. This disrupts traditional labor patterns at a much faster rate than it provides new job opportunities. The result is massive unemployment, the rise of the urban slums — marking the first stage in the migration process — and from there the mass movement to the center. These migrants rarely compete directly with native workers in the center; instead, a wholly new sector — what sociologist Alejandro Portes calls the immigrant enclave — is created for them.[11] Thus, dualization at the center reinforces, and is reinforced by, dualization in the periphery.

An important aspect of the regional cosmos is the rise of the cosmopolis — a major urban center that shifts from being a major metropolis of the center to being the metropolis of the entire regional cosmos. This is precisely the role that Miami has come to play in the West Atlantic regional cosmos.[12] Miami is no longer an American city: it is a West Atlantic city, more vital to, and more dependent on, the needs of the circum-Caribbean societies and cultures than it is on the other sectors of the U.S. economy. It is the political, cultural, social, and economic hub and heart of the Caribbean.

Culturally, the periphery is greatly influenced by the society of the center, but the reverse is also the case, as the example of reggae demonstrates. Another example of periphery-to-center cultural flows is the transmission of Spanish and Haitian creole, which has resulted not simply in the creation of a multilingual center where English once prevailed but, more broadly, in the Latinization of English and the Anglicization of Spanish. This process of creolization, in turn, has resulted in the creation of wholly new cultural forms in the transnational space, such as "New Yorican" and Miami Spanish.

The same process of cosmopolitan creolization can be found in other areas of culture: in the rapid spread of Spanish-American food, Franco-Haitian-American dishes, and the recent diffusion of the Jamaican "jerk" method of cooking in both Jamerican (Jamaican-American) and mainstream American cooking; in the Latin and West Indian carnivals that are now a standard part of the festivals of the cosmopolis; in the infusion and transformation of Afro-West Indian and Afro-Latin cults, whose animal sacrifices were recently offered constitutional protection by the Supreme Court after a major nativist challenge; in the ironic revival of the game of cricket, once an elite sport among the dominant Anglo-Americans, under the impact of the Afro-West Indian working-class immigrants; in the spread of the dreadlocks style of hair grooming among African Americans and, increasingly, among white Americans from the Jamaican Rastafarian immigrants. These are only some of the more visible expressions of this extraordinary process of periphery-induced creolization in the cosmopolis.

One of the most fascinating, and neglected, areas of cultural exchange between the cosmopolis and the West Atlantic periphery is in intellectual and professional life. The British, Spanish, and French academic and professional cultures have traditionally dominated the countries of the periphery, the result of their respective colonial experiences. The ruthlessly selective nature of these European traditions created intellectual cultures that were at once highly sophisticated and elitist. What emerged in the black Caribbean — a vibrant engagement with European intellectualism in which the culture of Europe was critically embraced, dissected, and reintegrated through the filter of a creolized neo-African sensibility and aesthetic — had no parallel on the American mainland. It was possible only because of the overwhelming demographic presence of blacks in the West Indies, in contrast with the minority status of blacks in the mainland cosmopolis. In the periphery, the neo-European culture of the elite was mediated through agents of the hegemonic powers, who were themselves black or light-skinned. Hence race, per se, was muted as a factor in the cultural conflict that accompanied the decolonization process.

The ironic effect was that the European experience could be adjudicated, and dialectically explored, in purely cultural terms, devoid of the confounding effects of racial segregation and rejection. In contrast with the black American condition, where any engagement with the dominant culture always ran the risk of the loss of racial identity and the fear of racial betrayal, resulting in an understandable rejection of all intellectualism, the West Indian intellectual developed a love-hate relationship with the culture of the "mother country" that was mediated through fellow blacks. The paradigmatic challenge in this situation became, not the rejection and suspicion of all intellectualism, but a desperate need to outdo the imperial culture at its own game. Intellectualism, however, went far beyond mere anti-imperial one-upmanship. For the ambitious black West Indian, it was, until recently, the only path to mobility, given the paucity of resources and the monopolization of the limited commercial positions by whites and Asians.

The net result has been a virtual hotbed of intellectualism among Afro-Caribbean peoples. These small, poor islands have, arguably, the highest per capita concentration of scholars, professionals, and real, as well as would-be, intellectuals as any place in the world. It is not Germany, Switzerland, or the United States that has produced the greatest proportion of Nobel laureates per thousand, but the tiny, dirt-poor island nation of St. Lucia. With an at-home population of under 100,000, it has produced two Nobel laureates, the economist Sir A. W. Lewis, and the poet Derek Walcott. Trinidad's V. S. Naipaul is generally considered one of the two or three best novelists writing in English. And they are merely the tip of the iceberg.

This extraordinary intellectual and professional tradition is now being rapidly incorporated into the West Atlantic cosmopolis. American educational aid has been accompanied by American models of education, transforming the elitist nature of these systems. At the same time, there has been a massive redirection of the flow of talent from the region. All roads no longer lead to the old colonial metropoles of London and Paris but increasingly to the great East Coast cosmopolitan centers. Budding West Indian intellectuals now experience their required period of creative exile, not in Europe, but in America, where many take up permanent residence. What is more, a disproportionate number of American academic and other professionals are of West Indian ancestry. Paralleling the cross-fertilization of African American lower-class popular culture by West Indian immigrants is the interaction of Afro-Caribbean and African American traditions within the cosmopolitan academe, which has significant implications not only for the cultures of both traditions but also for the wider culture of the cosmopolis.

The special contribution of West Indian intellectualism in the cosmopolitan context will be a transference of its distinctive strategy of aggressive engagement with the dominant tradition of neo-European civilization — a strategy that, at its worst, generates enormous identity crises and self-destructive emotional and physical violence, but at the same time, and at its best, is the crucible for the explosively competitive syncretism that finds expression in Rastafarianism and *voudon*, reggae and merengue, and negritude, magical realism, *omeros*, and the self-loathing genius of V. S. Naipaul. Such engagement African Americans have independently achieved so far only in the universalizing vitalism of rock music and the jazz aesthetic. My prediction is that the West Indian presence in the cosmopolis will act as a catalyst for the promotion of this transcendent Afro-European contribution to the emerging global culture.

In structural terms, the mass migration of peoples from the periphery in this new context of cheap transportation and communication has produced a wholly different kind of social system. The migrant communities in the center are not ethnic groups in the traditional American sense. In the interaction between center and periphery, the societies of the periphery are radically changed, but so is the traditional immigrant community of the center. What has emerged, from the viewpoint of the peripheral states, is distinctive transnational societies in which there is no longer any meaningful identification of political and social boundaries. Thus, more than one-half of the adult working populations of many of the smaller eastern Caribbean states now live outside of these societies, mainly in the immigrant enclaves of the United States. About 40 percent of all Jamaicans, and perhaps half of all Puerto Ricans, live outside of the political boundaries of these societies, mainly in America. The interesting thing about these communities is that their members feel as at home in the mainland segment as in the original politically bounded areas.

These communities are more like self-contained colonies — in this respect, they remind one of the *politeumata* of the Hellenistic cities — within the body politic of the United States, and it is a serious error to confuse them with the traditional ethnic communities, including native African Americans.

They are what the Jamaican folk poet, Louise Bennett, calls "colonization in reverse." The former colonies now become the mother country; the imperial metropolis becomes the frontier of infinite resources, only now the resources consist not simply of unexploited land but of underutilized deindustrializing capital and the postindustrial service and professional sectors. There is no traumatic transfer of national loyalty from the home country to the host polity, since home is readily accessible and national loyalty is a waning sentiment in what is increasingly a postnational world. Jamaican, Puerto Rican, Dominican, and Barbadian societies are no longer principally defined by the political-geographical units of Jamaica, Puerto Rico, the Dominican Republic, and Barbados but by *both* the populations and cultures of these units and their postnational colonies in the cosmopolis.

Other Regional Cosmoses

In addition to the West Atlantic system, there are at least three other emerging multinational spaces within the body politic of contemporary America: the Tex-Mex cosmos of the Southwest, incorporating northern Mexican and Southwestern Euro-Indian cultures, peoples, and economies; the Southern California cosmos, with its volatile, unblended mosaic of Latin, Asian, and Afro-European cultures; and the newly emerged Pacific Rim cosmos of the Northwest, which integrates the economies and bourgeois cultures of industrial Asia and traditional Euro-America.

While the processes of incorporation and creolization are broadly similar in all four regional cosmoses, they differ sharply in their degrees of integration; in the volume and velocity of cultural, economic, and demographic flows; in the levels of asymmetry in the transfer of ideas, cultural products, and skills; in the patterns and stages of creolization; and in the nature and extent of the social and cultural conflicts that inevitably accompany the process of cosmopolitanization.

On all these indices, the West Atlantic cosmos is, in my view, the most advanced, especially in the degree of integration and the extent to which the nation-state has been transcended as a major basis of collective commitment and constraint on livelihood. The major outlyers in this system are Haiti and Cuba, but in light of the already large contingent of Cubans and Haitians on the mainland, it is best to see their integration as a temporarily halted process, the one on ideological, the other on racist grounds. It is only a matter of time before both these restraints are eroded.

Next in level of integration is the Tex-Mex cosmos. Although it is the oldest of the four, the Tex-Mex cosmos is confined to a limited range of interactions and, in many respects, is the most asymmetric in its flows. The economic interaction consists largely of cheap, unskilled labor serving labor-intensive agricultural and light-industrial capital. Cultural flows are limited to popular music and the culinary arts. The hegemonic Anglo-American culture has remained strikingly oblivious to any significant Latinization. The architecture of the great cities of the region is aggressively Anglo-American, as is its professional and academic life, which takes account of the Latin presence in well-funded programs of Latin American and Latino studies.

The Southern California cosmos is the most heterogeneous and least integrated of the four and undoubtedly the most volatile. South and East Asian peoples of highly varied provenance meet Latin, Anglo-, and African Americans at all socioeconomic levels. Economic flows are complex, involving highly skilled, professional, and entrepreneurial Asians, professional and working-class Latinos, as well as blacks of all classes and hegemonic Anglo-Americans. There has, as yet, been surprisingly little cross-fertilization of cultures in the cosmos; the process of creolization remains mainly at the pidgin stage, in language as in other areas of culture. The cultural mix has been correctly described as a salad, and a thoroughly unappetizing one at that. That the nation's worst ethnic riot has recently taken place in this cosmos comes as no surprise. That the riot was not a traditional black-white conflict, as erroneously reported by the press, but a multiethnic conflagration engaging more Latinos than blacks, in spite of its origins in the police beating of a black man, Rodney King, is understandable in light of the extreme differences between the interacting cultures and classes.

The Pacific Rim cosmos is the newest, least complex, and potentially most integrated of the four systems. It is, in effect, the transnational space of the most advanced economic sectors of East Asia and the American mainland. Its boundaries in North America extend beyond the U.S. polity, incorporating the Canadian state of British Columbia.

The American Cosmos

What are the implications of all this for our understanding of contemporary America? I believe that it is best to conceive of not one, but three Americas — traditional America, multicultural America, and ecumenical America — a vast sociological cosmos bounded by a single, powerful polity. The three Americas are obviously related, but it is important not to confuse them, especially in discussions of multiculturalism.

Multicultural America is made up of the mainland or metropolitan populations of the four "transnational spaces" or regional cosmoses discussed above. It has been called immigrant America by Portes and others, and while this term obviously captures an important dimension of this sector, it is likely to be misleading to the degree that it invites too close a comparison with the immigrant America of earlier years. As I have pointed out, there is something fundamentally different in the relationship between these immigrant communities with both their home societies (to which they remain strongly linked socially and culturally) and the broader American society, with which they are permanently intertwined. Multicultural America is a great socio-cultural concourse, a space where all the cultures from the center's several regional cosmoses meet, resist, embrace, display their cultural wares at annual parades, gawk at, fight, riot, and learn to live with each other, sometimes even learn a little something from each other.

By traditional America, I mean the Euro-African world that emerged from the Puritan North, the industrial smokestacks, the prairie farms, and the slave South. It is the America of the Midwestern main street, of the old and new South, and of the ethnic working classes. It is the America of Richard Nixon, J. Edgar Hoover, and Louis Farrakhan. But it is also the America of

Jimmy Carter and the Congressional Black Caucus, of the land grant colleges and the United Negro Colleges. Socially, it is committed to enhanced opportunities and intergenerational mobility, but it is also historically racist, though changing in this regard, and profoundly separatist in its basic orientation. It embraces all races and classes, and today a great many African Americans are as committed to the separatist ideal as their Southern white counterparts. There has been some progress: instead of "separate and unequal," the ethic of this America, as a result of African American pressure, is now "separate but *truly* equal." There is profound disagreement about how such an America is to be achieved — witness the war over affirmative action — but all parties, except for the fringe extremists, are in agreement in their desire to live peacefully and separately.

Ironically, traditional America does have a common culture. At the elite level, it is largely the Anglo-American tradition modified by interactions with the older, more traditional ethnic groups, including mainstreaming African Americans, and by continental European influences. At the popular level, traditional America has been deeply influenced by the African American working class: in its language, music, art, and religion and in many of its attitudes. For a long time, it simply refused to acknowledge this influence, but in recent decades it has come to do so. It does so even while remaining committed to a separatist society, though one less and less rationalized in racist terms. The persisting racial segregation among black and white traditional Americans is today as much a product of class as of race and is in many ways more voluntary than imposed.

Perhaps the strongest unifying cultural feature of traditional America is its Christian heritage. Originally and still largely Protestant, traditional America is rapidly losing its hostility toward Catholicism, as an overriding convergence of conservative religious values becomes more important: the belief in a Christian God and regular churchgoing; the commitment to patriarchy; the demonization of abortion rights; the preference for punitive law-and-order forms of childrearing and justice; the neo-Puritan fear of sex; uncritical patriotism; reverence for, and for many, dependence on, the military; and the parochial suspicion of the foreign. Even while firmly settled in their separate communities, the many different white ethnic groups and the large core of working- and middle-class blacks who make up traditional America are fully committed to this still thriving system of values.

The Meaning of Race

In one important area, traditional America is under strong pressure from the multicultural sector to change one of its central values, namely, the meaning and conception, though not the significance, of race. Traditionally, race has been defined among both black and white Americans in binary terms: the so-called one-drop rule sociologically excluded any intermediary racial groups on a continuum between blacks and whites. While the binary rule was originally constructed and rigidly imposed by whites out of their commitment to notions of racial purity and exclusion, it is one that traditional African Americans have come to embrace for political and cultural reasons. The rule operated with extraordinary tenacity not only because both the traditional "races" came to accept it, but because later immigrant groups quickly conformed. Jews, dark-skinned southern Europeans, and Caucasoid Hispanics, once rejected as "true whites," eagerly struggled for, and eventually won, acceptance within the Caucasian chalk circle of white people — in contrast with the excluded blacks, whose presence is required for the extraordinary valorization of whiteness. (The point is best made by noting that for the average Irishman in nonblack Ireland, whiteness has no social meaning; Ireland is, in fact, one of the least racist of European societies, as any well-traveled African American or West Indian tourist will attest; however, whiteness is instantly embraced as a valued social, cultural, and economic asset by the marginal, socially insecure Irish immigrant in America, as the well-documented historical negrophobia of working-class Irish Americans, their liberal politics nothwithstanding, will also readily attest.)

The rise of the multicultural sector strongly undermines the binary rule in two important respects: one demographic, the other cultural. One reason why the binary rule worked so well was that African Americans were, by and large, the only significant "other" in the American population for most of the nation's history. Until recently, Asians and dark-skinned Latin and South Asian immigrants were an insignificant demographic presence; and Native Americans — who up to the end of the eighteenth century constituted the second significant racial "other" — were removed from consideration through decimation and confinement on reservations.

All this has changed dramatically with the rise of the regional cosmos and the multicultural sector. Visibly nonwhite Asians and Latin Americans, who by no stretch of the imagination can be socially redefined and incorporated within the social category of "white people," now exist in significant numbers in the society; indeed, they will outnumber blacks by the turn of the century. Since these groups are clearly neither whites nor blacks, a serious crisis of racial definition now confronts those clinging to the binary conception of race.

Quite apart from the purely demographic factor, however, is the cultural refusal of most of the new immigrants to play by the binary rule, as early streams of immigrants have done. On the one hand, most of the new Asian immigrants have a strong sense of their own racial identity, are proud of the way they look, and do not wish to be redefined racially as anything else. And this sense of racial pride is further reinforced by the multicultural celebration of ethno-racial differences. On the other hand, most immigrants from Latin America bring with them, in addition to their racial heterogeneity, their own highly developed nonbinary or "interval-type" notions of race. That is, socially significant distinctions are made among persons on a continuum between obviously black and obviously white persons. A visibly nonwhite, but light- or brown-skinned Puerto Rican, Dominican, Jamaican, or Brazilian does not consider himself "black." One only has to observe the elaborate shade gradations and mating and marriage patterns of Cuban, Puerto Rican, and other Latin immigrants to recognize that a wholly different principle of racial classification is at play. A similar nonbinary pattern prevails among South Asians between black-skinned "Dravidian" types and fair-skinned "Aryan" types. And the same holds for East Asians. Indeed, nonbinary racial classification is the norm among the vast majority of non-European peoples.

Added to these two factors is a third challenge to the binary rule: the preeminence of Japan as a major economic power. The coincidence of the advanced industrial world with the white world strongly reinforced notions of racial purity and superiority. The challenge to American and European economic hegemony from a clearly nonwhite power, one that until as late as the 1960s was castigated as the "yellow peril," its immigrants unashamedly herded into concentration camps during the Second World War, has created confusion for traditional Americans holding fast to their binary notion of race. When one adds to this the out-performance of whites in the educational system by the former "yellow devils" — especially on I.Q. tests, which have functioned so prominently as a "scientific" justification for the binary, purist dogma — it is easy to understand why the binary rule is now in crisis.

Ecumenical America

Ecumenical America is not merely cosmopolitan, for it goes beyond the simple embrace of many cultures maintaining their separate identities. It is, rather, the universal culture that emerged and continues to develop in the great cities and university towns of the nation. This culture is a genuinely ecumenical one: it draws from everywhere, not just from the local cultures of the traditional ethnic and immigrant sectors and the traditional Euro-American culture at its doorstep. The image of the melting pot fails to describe the process by which it emerges, for it does not indiscriminately absorb all and everything into some common stew. There is a complex process of selection and universalization of particular cultural forms and styles generating its great cultural innovations for itself and for the world: in science, technology, literature, dance, painting, music, and cuisine.

Like traditional America, it has both a formal or elite and a popular or vernacular level. English, both of the streets and the academy, is its common language. Its shared art thrives in the works of a Jasper Johns or an Andy Warhol (with their ironic ecumenization of traditional America's most beloved icons) but, perhaps most quintessentially, in the musical form of jazz. On the popular level, the shared art of ecumenical America is also strongly influenced by African Americans. Increasingly, the products of the regional cosmoses are selected out for universalization, as in the ecumenization of Chinese and Mexican cuisine, the poetry of Derek Walcott, the fiction of Saul Bellow and Maxine Hong Kingston, and the drama of Eugene O'Neill. Ecumenical America also draws directly from the wider world in meeting the needs of its art and its technology. The culture it produces, in turn, has become the koine, or common currency, of the world, the first genuinely global culture on the face of the earth.

Ecumenical America is based primarily in the postindustrial economy, with its advanced technological plants, complex services, and multinational corporations. It is no utopia, as the legion of previously secure unemployed workers and managers of the smokestack industrial regions and rapidly obsolescent high-tech sectors can attest. It is almost as class-ridden as traditional America. Politically, it is mainly liberal, but it includes the politically very conservative elites and middle managers of the multinational corporations and silicon suburbs. It also includes the elite managers, scientists, and intellectuals from all over the world — Indian engineers, Japanese and Hong Kong businessmen, Argentinean doctors, European managers and artists, and Caribbean intellectuals — who enter this sector at the top and are not to be confused with the working-class or sweatshop entrepreneurs of the immigrant enclave economy.

A New Cultural Policy

Let me conclude with a few reflections on the kind of cultural policy that this interpretation of the American cosmos implies. In the first place, it seems to me that any attempt at a single policy for all of America is a nonstarter. Any cultural policymaker must begin by recognizing the fundamentally tripartite nature of America. It is a waste of time trying to persuade a traditional American to embrace a Robert Mapplethorpe; it might even be unreasonable. The most we can reasonably expect is that he or she respect the right of ecumenical Americans to view Mapplethorpe's photographs publicly.

Second, it should now be clear that the multicultural social philosophy and approach to the arts and culture is wholly inadequate for the American cosmos. It very adequately addresses the needs of immigrant or multicultural America but is inappropriate as a strategy for the other two cultural systems that embrace the vast majority of Americans.

Indeed, it is questionable whether there can be a single policy even for the multicultural sector itself. In the first place, as we have seen, the American, cosmopolitan parts of the four regional cosmoses that together constitute the social bases of multicultural America are at different stages of development, especially in their degrees of integration. What holds true for the highly integrated West Atlantic cosmos, with its harmonizing processes of creolization, simply does not apply to the fissiparous Southern California cosmos.

But there is a more profound problem with regard to any attempt at a single multicultural policy. This is the inherent self-contradiction of all programs that adhere to the dogma of relativism. If all ideals, all values, and all art in all cultures and subcultures are of equal worth, there is no basis for the view that relativism — the basic value of the multicultural theorists and policy advocates — is of any greater worth than the basic values of any of the celebrated subcultures that deny the worth of others — including that of the relativists — in absolutist terms. Relativism requires the acceptance of its condemnation by the very antirelativists it embraces. This is no academic abstraction, as Americans have already learned in the course of their current bitter culture wars. A multicultural relativist is in no position to condemn the traditionalist fundamentalist's insistence that not only is the Christian God the only true God, but that no one has the right to prevent his children from attending public schools where the day begins and ends with Christian prayers. Similarly, a black nationalist has no moral basis for condemning a white supremacist. Indeed, partly out of recognition of this contradiction, there has been an astonishing recent convergence of interests between several white and black racist nationalists. The present volatile debate over speech codes, and more generally, over the First Amendment, is disturbing testimony to the potentially catastrophic social and cultural implications of an unthinking commitment to the self-contradictions of the relativistic dogma that is basic for multiculturalist theorists.

Traditional America is inherently hostile to such a strategy and rightly complains of its disregard for a common center. In its extreme commitment to relativism, multiculturalism well serves the needs of immigrant peoples and cultures thrown upon each other and who must learn basic principles — often contrary to their own traditions — of tolerance for others. But discrimination is the essence of cultural creation, and this same relativism, when applied to the other two areas of the American cosmos, could be deadening in its impact.

The multicultural ideology, then, is certainly needed, but its limits must be understood. Making it the American creed would be a serious mistake. In general, art within the immigrant sector should be encouraged, preferably by private foundations rather than the government, but only where it looks toward, and strives to become, a part of the shared art of the ecumene. However, where the immigrant artist is atavistic, looking only back at his or her original culture, he or she should be tolerated, respected, and accepted in good faith, but not actively supported. It is not the business of the ecumenical to promote the atavistic.

Ecumenical America is no utopia. Nonetheless, it seems clear to me that this is the future of America, for better or for worse. There is no basis for the commonly heard criticism that associates the ecumenical with a grey, homogenized world. Nor is there any justification for the view that the ecumenical is dominated by a global financial elite having no responsibility to any local community. The ultimate thrust of the ecumenical is indeed transnational and, in many respects, postnational. But this is the way of the world in the twenty-first century, and such postnational orientation is by no means confined to the financial elite. Indeed, as I have shown, it is the migrant peasants, working classes, and intellectuals from the periphery of the world's transnational spaces who are most postnational in their attitudes and behavior. The typical Jamaican resident of Brooklyn or Mexican resident of Texas has already gone far beyond any transnational capitalist of New York in his or her attitudes, migratory movements, and life-style.

We have no choice but to accept the inevitable, but we do have choices in what we make of it. Ecumenical America and its advocates, among whom I count myself, should recognize its special place, not only as the most advanced part of the American cosmos but as the vital source of the world's first truly global culture. It should support artists, scientists, and other cultural creators in and out of America whose work resonates and who are dialectically engaged with the emerging shared art and shared ways of the global ecumene, at both the advanced and vernacular levels of social and cultural life.

Notes

1. Alan Lomax, *Folk Song Style and Culture* (Washington, D.C.: American Association for the Advancement of Science, 1968).

2. Paul E. Willis, *Common Culture* (Boulder, Colo.: Westview, 1990), 26.

3. For the standard Frankfurt School criticisms, see Theodor W. Adorno, *Introduction to the Sociology of Music* (New York: Continuum, 1988) and Herbert Marcuse, *One-Dimensional Man* (Boston: Beacon, 1964).

4. Peter Manuel, *Popular Musics of the Non-Western World* (New York: Oxford University Press, 1988), 20.

5. Deanna Robinson, Elizabeth Buck et al., *Music at the Margins: Popular Music and Global Cultural Diversity* (Newbury Park, Calif.: Sage, 1991), 4.

6. Orlando Patterson, "The Dance Invasion of Britain: On the Cultural Diffusion of Jamaican Popular Arts," *New Society*, No. 207 (September 1966).

7. See Simon Jones, *Black Culture, White Youth* (Basingstoke: Macmillan Education, 1988).

8. See Stephen Davis and Peter Simon, *Reggae Bloodlines* (New York: De Capo, 1979).

9. See Saskia Sassen, *The Mobility of Labor and Capital* (New York: Cambridge University Press, 1988).

10. For a detailed analysis of this cosmos, see my essay, "The Emerging West Atlantic System: Migration, Culture, and Underdevelopment in the U.S. and Caribbean," in *Population in an Interacting World*, ed. William Alonso (Cambridge, Mass.: Harvard University Press, 1987).

11. Alejandro Portes and Rubén G. Rumbout, *Immigrant America* (Berkeley: University of California Press, 1990).

12. For a spirited journalistic tour of this regional cosmos and Miami's central role in it, see Joel Garreau, *The Nine Nations of North America* (Boston: Houghton Mifflin, 1981), 167–206.

Chapter 13

Melting Down the
Iron Suits of History

Stanley Crouch

In the Western Hemisphere, in the Americas, ours is too often a condition of mutual resentment, from the bottom to the top, from the top to the bottom, and it informs some of the most sour melodies of our dialogue. Those who suffer from one form or another of underdevelopment speak of an ever-stinging exploitation that has pulsated since the conquistadors. They talk about having been systematically abused and excluded, continually held down in the wretched mud of injustice. The better-off perceive this as bellyaching and are sure, no matter the apparent accuracy of the statistics, that it all breaks down to wanting the opportunity to get even with the descendants of those who smacked cold the civilizations of the indigenous peoples and slowly built a civilization beyond what any could have imagined.

I term these themes of mutual resentment "The Iron Suits of History." The term was inspired by *The Man in the Iron Mask*. In that French novel by the mulatto Alexandre Dumas, we are told the story of one identical twin imprisoning the other in a hard, metal disguise in order to make impossible the recognition of their brotherhood, their mutual origin. Fear of losing power to the other, fear of being replaced, was the motive. The mask was a symbol of battle, and he who ended up with his features hidden from view had lost.

In our time, we want to hide the whole form of the opposition, not just the face. We want the twin closed in from head to foot. We can then walk around this stationary figure and point out all of the things we don't like. Assuming the pompous moral superiority that comes with the mantle of the victim, we accuse the man in the iron suit of disrupting our innocence, shooting trouble upward or showering it down. We bitterly assert that pastoral societies at one with nature were destroyed by the collision with superior technology. Or we counter by claiming how endangered sophisticated societies are by the onrush of former barbarians who respect neither our highly evolved codes of hierarchy nor the well-worn paths of preparation. What we are all trying to do when we stoop down into that sort of resentful rhetoric is make a getaway. We are trying to slip past the unwieldy demands of modern life, that life in which we have extended our imaginations, our high-mindedness, our needs, our shortsightedness, our fears, and our ruthlessness through machines that speak for us and against us. In effect, as we try to duck the democratic invention called for by our wacky world, we are hustling iron suits.

The trouble with iron suits is that they keep us, as they say in the blues, sinking down. What we need now is an elevating but unsentimental vision. It has to be high-minded and tough enough to match the endless miscegenations so responsible for giving the New World such a marvelous and messy gathering of styles and societies. If we speak only from positions of resentment and paranoia, we resist the plucky sophistication that our time calls for, this era in which satellite dishes and international trade continue to make all of us more and more parts of each other. Through the power of electronic mass media, we now routinely see each other in celebration, protest, wealth, destitution, plague, war, corruption, scandal, athletic competition, beauty pageants, decadence, and so on. Our economies swell or contract on the basis of how well we traverse the various obstacles to international competition for the appetites of consumers worldwide. It matters little at this point what any national leader says when attacking the external competitors: If they make better tools or creature comforts, the people of his country will ignore him whenever their purchasing power allows. The better mousetrap now seeks not to kill the mouse but to keep him buying.

So loyalty to quality and innovation, and to the shifting mysteries of mass tastes, now transcends any feeling of obligation to domestic products. The car manufacturers of Detroit, Michigan, learned that a long time ago, as did the makers of electronic consumer products in the United States. Their laughing first at the Volkswagen bug and later dismissing Sony didn't matter much to the drivers of cars and the buyers of stereo equipment. One car manufacturing executive in Detroit observed — gee whiz! — that they were all surprised when the opportunity to buy at a bargain gave way to the opportunity to get a better made car. No one could remain in business by assuming the locals would forever be yokels incapable of determining which goods gave the most utilitarian pleasure. That phenomenon constitutes, ultimately, an economic extension of the miscegenations that now define the modern world. Mixtures of technological innovations and refinements course into the cultural blood-streams of human society at large just as they have for centuries in the Western Hemisphere, where European, African, Hispanic, and Asian factors have been boiling an increasingly thick gumbo, a gumbo made differently in many places, but a gumbo nonetheless. It is the continual motion away from any restrictive sense of purity that gives us our various identities, creates our dilemmas, and enriches our sense of human variety and human folly.

Sacrifice and Massacre

It is quite easy to say such things and be mistaken for one who would deny the tragedy so elemental to the very creation of the New World. Though the Vikings made a short run into North America, it was the arrival of

Christopher Columbus and Hernán Cortés that began the making of what we now know as the Americas. Those arrivals let loose the demons of conquest, mass slaughter, and destruction. As Tzvetan Todorov discusses in *The Conquest of America*, the scale of exploitation and casual slaughter suffered by the Indians at the hands of the Spaniards seems to predict what we saw enacted again with such might and rapacious certitude during World War II that an international tribunal at Nuremberg coined the term "crimes against humanity" to describe the unbridled barbarism of the Third Reich. Our looking back to the point at which our hemisphere began its travail into the modern world on the pikes of conquest means something quite different from what we might have preferred to imagine at some other time. The repulsive blood sports of the conquistadors are made far less distant by our familiarity with totalitarian purges or the genocidal wars of Bosnia and Africa that presently chill and break the world heart. The historical boomerang returns not only with yellowed and grim statistics but with fresh blood.

Yet the founding of a Spanish colonial extension with the edge of a sword was not new, even if it did take place in the New World. The midnight darkness of history is filled with mass graves or corpses left to bloody the teeth of scavengers. Most societies begin, as Saul Bellow observes, with injustice — forcing of others away from desired land or into submission under an order asserted through the tools and brutalities of war. Once murder during hand-to-hand combat or surprise attack is established as basic, many things become almost inevitable. Pillaging, rape, torture, mass executions, slaughters of the innocent have a predictability so broad we can observe them, to greater or lesser degrees, on both sides in almost any bitter struggle.

Todorov writes of the Spanish wars of conquest in the Western Hemisphere

Unlike sacrifices, massacres are generally not acknowledged or proclaimed; their very existence is kept secret and denied. This is because their social function is not recognized, and we have the impression that such action finds its justification in itself: One wields the saber for the pleasure of wielding the saber; one cuts off the Indian's nose, tongue, and penis without this having any ritual meaning for the amputator.

We must also acknowledge that the civilizations laid low by the Spaniards were themselves no Sunday afternoon strolls through the park. Though, for instance, the manners in the court of the Aztecs were recognized by the conquistadors as more refined than any they had seen in Europe, the Aztecs were also colonizers, equally at ease with bloodletting. They knew no innocence that stopped short of the stone, sacrifical knife, and the huge pits filled with the bodies of virgins. Moreover, there is a distinction between the often arbitrary, even playful, bloodlust of the Spaniards and the severe rituals in which many thousands of their own were sacrificed by the Indians in order to appease the local gods. In the actions of the conquistadors, we see the suspension of Western morality, the kinds of brutal acts allowed in some remote place where the law is only vaguely acknowledged. Massacre is thus intimately linked to colonial wars waged far from the metropolitan country.

But Todorov helps us see that we can move beyond the historical sentimentality that builds iron suits only when the critical sword of evaluation cuts both ways. Todorov raises a question that encapsulates the stern and simultaneously empathetic quality of modern assessment at its finest. He asks, "But what if we do not want to have to choose between a civilization of sacrifice and a civilization of massacre?"

Our Miscegenated Identity

We understand the enormous price paid by the indigenous peoples of the Western Hemisphere only — I repeat, *only*— because we now live in a world where the idea of a transcendent humanity developed into a vision of national and international social policy as a result of the Enlightenment. At our very best, we do not believe that there is any justification for random and sadistic violence by representatives of the state, even conquering soldiers, because ours is now a world of complete human identification. Differences of language, religion, color, culture, and so on — no matter how initially strange to us — have ceased to justify the brutal methods of immoral conduct. This is the moral conscience of democracy. It is what fires our evangelical concerns with world starvation and world health, the feeding of starving children, innoculation, water purification, rescue missions, and all that is done by professionals and volunteers in the interest of lessening the burdens of degradation. That is why the rights of animals and the environment itself are argued in our time with the intensity once brought to slavery, women's suffrage, and child labor.

It is our miscegenated identity as Americans that brings all of those things together and allows us to understand where we fit in the whirlwind of modern life. We have been inside each other's bloodstreams, pockets, libraries, kitchens, schools, theaters, sports arenas, dance halls, and national boundaries for so long that our mixed-up and multiethnic identity extends from European colonial expansion and builds upon immigration. That identity now seems a prediction of what the Europe of the future may resemble, given the arrival of so many Africans, Asians, and Arabs into its nations. As each mother country now lies down with the former colonials, the guest workers, and the refugees, we see complex contemporary variations on the serfs who left the feudal manors and began living the independent lives that provided fresh labor and gave shape to European cities centuries ago. In short, big gumbo pots on the other side of the Atlantic are now boiling again. Of course, there are those hysterics in Europe who see this mixture as a murderous, blinding, and suicidal curse of Oedipal dimension, an opening of the boudoir to crippled barbarians once properly left to die on the hills of underdevelopment. When they lament a loss of "identity" or cry out for "authenticity," they are perhaps suggesting that the Sphinx of colonial detention should never have gone down in flames. We in the Americas should know better. We have already been there.

On this side of the world, we are still arguing over immigration, trade, race relations, gender politics, sexual preferences, the environment, and national debt, but we have a common identity and a common set of conflicts resulting from relationships so intertwined we couldn't recognize ourselves if we were somehow to awake from sleep in a "pure" state. It is because of our miscenegated presence in the Americas that the ideas of the Enlightenment were so thoroughly enriched, so inclusively stretched beyond the idea that all Europeans had a human commonality precluding language, religion, and national boundaries. The indigenous Indian, the Spanish and Indian mixture that became the Hispanic, the African who became the Negro American slave and also added another strain to the Hispanic, the Asians who arrived to help build the continental railroad, and every other variant of human ancestry pushed the democratic ideal further always from provincialism. In the Western Hemisphere, people who carried within their bloodstreams the nations of the world supplied — through their countless achievements in every arena of endeavor — all necessary proof of infinite human possibility. That proof became the debating mortar of definition which holds together the increasingly different mixtures of bricks that form the entire cultural edifice of the Americas.

The Double-Edged Swords of Judgment

None of this has come about without the wounds so deeply scraped inside the iron suits of history and the blood that softens the earth on which we stand, suggesting to some that apocalyptic quicksand is our only future. I don't think that is the case. We need now to temper our dialogue with the stern and empathetic assessment grounded in the sophistication and toughness of the democratic vision at its least sentimental. Our job is to melt down the iron suits fitted for us by those who see history as no more than a melodramatic duel between the good guys and the bad guys. Some want to imprison the Western World and capitalism in an imperial iron suit by using the lock and key Edward Said calls "a politics of blame." Others have their own line of iron suits. They believe that those descended from innately less sophisticated oral societies are doomed by their genes or their class limitations and will never do more than impose burdens, ineptitude, and disorder on the civilized world.

Those are the two most dangerous tendencies in our contemporary world because they are religions of bad faith. The cataloguing of atrocities of the powerful or the scurrilous crimes of the slum dwellers proves nothing about the limitations of specific groups — or classes — within the democratic struggle; it only designates the challenges that lay before our humanity and our social structures. I am talking specifically about democracy because the true iron suit that sank into the mud made by its infliction of lies and ever larger wounds was Marxism. The toppling from nation to nation of the statues of Lenin expressed the outrage against closed societies in which human beings were no more than aspects of mathematics casually to be placed behind the minus signs of murder in order to prove out the correctness of theory.

Let us maintain that double-edged sword of assessment and face up to the economic religion of commerce that deifies the market as an invincible god of production and consumption, a world spirit that hovers over goods and finance, perpetually moving to realize itself in mysterious expansions and contractions. Well, it is and it isn't. There are captains as well as pirates of industry, each group including individuals sometimes too interchangeable to make us comfortable. We in the United States, which is the most successful commercial culture in the history of the world, maintain a running battle with the most corrupt manifestations of capitalism. We are familiar with scandals involving government contracts, price-fixing, insider trading, the intentional sale of dangerously shoddy products, money laundering, and the rest of it.

Yet that battle doesn't so much prove the fundamental evil of capitalism as it actually reveals a more fundamental aspect of the human struggle against folly, corruption, and mediocrity, the ageless demons that transcend all social and economic structures. After all, didn't we discover, even behind the barbed wire curtains of the totalitarian Marxist regimes, that the fires of theft, privilege, favoritism, greed, abuses of power, and corruption rose as high in their stench as they ever have any place else in the world? The central virtue of democracy, however, is that it is founded in individual liberty under the rule of law and the vigilant suspicion of power, which means continuous scrutiny and the eternal stuggle to purify the relationships between the people and the law, the people and the business sector, the people and the elected government.

We must maintain allegiance to that struggle in order to face up to our many dilemmas, one of which is the position of secret espionage in our political lives. It is not news to us that the strategies created within smoke-filled rooms have led to the propping up of one dictator after another, the financing of death squads, deals with totalitarians involved in the international drug trade, disruptions of economies to speed the fall of political adversaries, assassinations, and a long list of known and as yet unknown deals that could swamp the soil of democracy, endangering the whole structure — were it not for the institutionalized freedom of that all-important scrutiny as well as the right of critical redress through protest, investigative journalism, voting, and governmental response.

Those key elements prove and expand upon Thomas Jefferson's observation that the tree of liberty is periodically watered with blood, not always the blood of domestic patriots but just as significantly the blood of those in other countries whose suffering reveals the culpability of irresponsible people publicly or secretly functioning within the power structure of democracy itself. Scrutiny and redress allow us to pull the covers of false patriotism off those who would use thug methods while pretending to protect us and hold dear our highest ideals. Such fundamental democratic freedoms make it possible for us to redeem ourselves through new policies and bring about vast change short of violent revolution.

In the ongoing democratic struggle, revolution always takes place in terms of policy, for ours is an experimental and improvising form in which serious data supplies us with proof of our successes, our partial successes, and our failures. Our ideas must meet the measure of our accomplishments. Our actions must stand up to our assessments. But, by our very nature as human beings, we are destined to the periodic descents which religion, literature, and philosophy attribute to our frailty in the face of our ideals.

Democracy is the myth of Sisyphus extended to that exciting and terrifying creation of the amusement park, the roller coaster, that ride in which the rising and falling illusion of imminent destruction is checked and balanced by the precision of the engineering. The grandeur of democratic precision is found in its foreseeing and accepting the fact that we must always be prepared slowly and painfully to chug up out of the inevitable valleys created by our least attractive human drives. That is not a defeatist cynicism; it is a cynicism of engagement. Democracy is a vision, as I say, which is undaunted by the imperfectability of humankind, its folly, its corruption, its mediocrity.

This does not mean that the sins stretching from the top to the bottom, from the bottom to the top, can be washed away with a mighty river of high-minded eloquence, but it does mean that we can seek to avoid repeating or sustaining the failures of an arrogant or sentimental past. In order to do this, we must reassert a confidence in the development of a democratic maturity that recognizes the rigors and subtleties of sophistication as the most refined manifestations of vitality.

The way that the iron suits of bad faith function currently within the United States can serve as a concluding example of the strange, colliding events that shake us out of all forms of innocence but also create some of the weirdest alliances — balling together protest, education, commerce, fads, and criminality. These alliances mirror the finest processes of democratic redress and acculturation but actually obscure and threaten democratic clarity.

The Corruption of Protest

Let us first step down into the valley. Rising from below has come a now-established disdain for the complexities of our democratic tasks. That disdain began in protest against the many ways the ideals of the Enlightenment were distorted by xenophobia, fear, and exploitation. In the United States, this disdain has evolved into the profession of alienation and complaint. These professional complainers profit from the fact that protest has become a commodity, and they move to manipulate us through our own reservations about power and our democratic willingness to listen to the other side, whether that other side is a composite of political, racial, and sexual criticism or is no more than the expression of the anxieties and insecurities of youth.

The profession of complaint and alienation is joined at the hip to youth rebellion and has dissonantly hammered out the shape of its iron suit on the anvil of bad faith and protest. Those hammerings ring out from destruction of the Civil Rights Movement by Black Power, from the international protests against the Vietnam War, from the romance of Third World Marxist revolution, from the Woodstock Nation's expression of a contemptuous, even desperate, cultural rejection of racism, of bourgeois suffocation, of imperial world politics through the celebration of sex, of drugs, of rock and roll. All those dissonant hammerings were given their sour harmonic resolution by the Watergate scandal, which was interpreted as unarguable proof of every extreme and defeatist political criticism. Watergate supposedly made obvious the fact that the system was so rotted by religiously devout corruption that only fools could ever believe in it again.

Nope. The Watergate scandal actually proved the reverse of every charge founded in the belief that the ruthless men hiding behind the ideals of American democracy were above the reproach of getting the bum's rush, the hand in the collar and the boot in the backside. Many arrogant men fell, and even Richard Nixon had to resign and take a helicopter out of town, whirling away in humiliation. No matter, the Watergate revelations sufficed to help institutionalize the profession of alienation, which presently spreads itself out from our academies to the world of popular culture and back. This profession is a kind of perversion of the role of inspector, those hired to reduce the possibilities of disaster from poor workmanship in, say, automobiles and airplanes. But unlike those inspectors, these professional complainers are barely concerned — if concerned at all — with improving the quality of our democratic life but are concerned with the profitable ironies of careers under capitalism, which make possible new occupations as fresh areas of endeavor open up.

It amounts to the corruption of protest, which we who study history know is no less vulnerable than anything else. As Octavio Paz observed in *One Earth, Four or Five Worlds:*

Previous generations had seen the cult of the terrible Father, adored and feared: Stalin, Hitler, Churchill, De Gaulle. In the decade of the sixties, an ambiguous image, alternately angry and orgiastic — the Sons — displaced the saturnine Father. We went from the glorification of the solitary old man to the exaltation of the juvenile tribe.

The ethos of the exalted tribe is provided by the professors of alienation. On campuses across the United States, these supposedly radical teachers who butter their bread by ranting against the Western World and Western History usually reduce all subjects of discussion to justifications for a sloppy rhetoric of blame posing as uplift of the oppressed and a reinvigoration of democratic discourse. They pretend to have appropriated the criticism of bourgeois education, the academic sophistication that is essential to broadening and refining of information and interpretation. Instead, these so often inferior scholars are only interested in maintaining their jobs by ranting that non-white students, women, and homosexuals will never get an even break.

Now and again they are exposed, but their power is that of academic entertainers who trade in resentment. They play upon the guilt of those in authority and the insecurity of their students, who are told that they will always be oppressed and that they run the danger of either being indoctrinated in self-hatred or remade into instruments of oppression. As homemade parlor pinks, these teachers have no interest in the real complexities of the world. As campus colonial chieftains, they don't engage in genuine intellectual exchange. Instead, they accept the trinkets of tenure and segregated departments while supplying the goods and rituals of cardboard "identity" that keep the provincials quiet. Their incompetence, half truths, wretched scholarship, and exquisite opportunism make it easier to dismiss the truly penetrating criticisms of our system.

Another aspect of the exalted tribe is present in the arena of feminism, which has been one of the most important movements toward our realizing the full potential of our society. The rhetoric of contemporary feminism has been vulnerable to cynical appropriation at least since a succession of famous women began posing nude in men's magazines and writing texts in which they described their layouts as ways of asserting themselves beyond the dictates of sexist exploitation! In popular culture, a figure like Madonna represents yet another vulgarizing corruption. She floozily sits atop a trend in which one female singer or group after another confuses pornography with liberation. In such work, sluttishness purports to be a manifesto. Young women are given the impression that their freedom comes not from getting respect as three-dimensional individuals but from brazenly embodying the kind of bimbo image in which the free-lance prostitute who defiantly refuses to work for a pimp is made a symbol of freedom. It is another commodity of false rebellion, one whose fans fail to realize that even the scummiest pornographers have always presented themselves as defenders of free expression, when in fact they have done nothing but shrink the complexities of romance and eroticism to a set of lurid cliches. The rights of a Madonna or a Larry Flynt are not abridged by our realizing who and what they are. They are not rebels; they are actually hard-core conformists.

Rewarding Raps

Quite obviously, the rebellion commodity appeals to adolescent anxiety as expressed through the language, clothing, and rituals of the outsider. In the mid-1950s the leather-jacketed biker arrived, wearing his hair greasy. He was an urban outlaw development of the young, antisocial cowboy, the roar of his motorcycle a technological extension of the horse galloping away from the impositions of civilization. That was the epoch when adolescence was institutionalized as a golden moment before the looming iron suit of adulthood.

During the 1960s, the intellectual pretensions of men like Allen Ginsberg and Bob Dylan gave a hard and bittersweet glaze to the candied apples of an Eden young people were told they could return to by boldly embracing their primitive urges and throwing off every corruption and repression foisted on them by the sterile, greedy, and racist adult world. At one point, there was a rejection of money and an attempt to make everything communal and free of charge. That didn't last very long at all, but the possibilities of huge profit through the sale of alienation made louder and louder by rock and roll electricity grew beyond what anyone could ever have predicted. That mass commercial element was what endured.

The most hostile form of youth rebellion, like all others, is now little more than a set of products inextricably connected to and promoted by the very world of big business and middle-aged executives it pretends to hate. This video theater of anger for sale, just like the second-rate professors of alienation, would be an utter failure if the institutions it professes to repudiate were suddenly to fold. As proselytized through the mass media of radio and cable television, such rebellion doesn't challenge the quality of big business; it submits to its most irresponsible tendency — the worship of the market god of profit, no matter the quality or the effect of the product.

Because such increasingly minor talents are able to become such big stars, the horizons of democratic success are reduced to the large salaries that come of promoting an urban version of a yowling Peter Pan backed up by a din of electrified cliches. This combination of anger, aggressive bad taste, nihilism, orgiastic frenzy, and the cults of the foul-mouthed hard rocker and the equally vulgar but even more antisocial gangster rapper tumble from the scourge of MTV, which broadcasts twenty-four hours a day into more and more overseas markets.

These trends do not supply sufficient responses to the disorder of our times; they help intensify that disorder. This is not a criticism of the essentially meaningless — and expected — bad taste and sentimentality of the adolescent fads that dominate pop music. Those pop tunes provide the maudlin soundtracks and anthems for young love, express through their nose-thumbing the difficulties of developing an identity, and supply the ground-beats for the communal releases of energy we always observe in the hard partying that offers momentary refuge from the demands of the approaching adult world of work. In the commodity of antisocial pop, however, what might once have been given its direction by the enthralling gallantry, earthiness, human insights, and communal lyricism of the very best blues has been reduced to combative squawking in the illiterate jargon of the black thug. Its racial developments are harrowing. We observe the white captains of media industry profiting from the marketing of the ethos of the black pirates of the streets.

In the world of gangster rap, the bone-headed Malcolm X's popularization of the rhetorical phrase "by any means necessary" has been removed from the world of saber-rattling racial politics and pushed into the arena of crime. It is the ruling philosophy of those for whom the accumulation of money and power is an end that validates murderous emulation of the Mafia strategies we even see flowering the world over, even ominously rising like a bloody-encrusted phoenix from the ashes of the gangster politics that once ruled Soviet Russia. Rap videos celebrate oversized gold and diamond jewelry, the endless guzzling of beer, the constant smoking of reefers, a bragging, impersonal, and promiscuous sexuality that refuses to go beyond the glands. Thug rappers chant out the most trivial reasons imaginable for committing acts of violence in order to "get some respect." Not even minstrelsy reiterated so ardently such racist stereotypes.

The adored and feared terrible father Octavio Paz spoke of has now been replaced within the exalted tribe by the naively admired black sociopath, the gangster whose "street knowledge" supposedly expresses the truest, least miscegenated version of black culture — "the real deal." This is the ultimate extension of the romantic love of the outlaw, the bad boy, the nihilist, he who lives at the fantasy center of rock and roll anger. Snarling racial alienation is now but one more item on the adolescent shopping list. The suburban white kid doesn't have to apply for a passport, put on a pith helmet, get innoculations, purchase expensive plane tickets, hire a guide, or buy mosquito netting. All he or she has to do is go to the record shop or turn on MTV. The alienated white adolescent then symbolically reaches down to pat the cap turned backwards on the head of the black commodity that has expressed "rock and roll anarchy" to a fare-thee-well. Ivory and ebony, ebony and ivory. They have worked it out.

The gangster rapper is an even less articulate variation on the so easily corrupted Black Panthers, a 1960s' group of thugs with Marxist revolutionary pretensions who successfully cowed middle-class, well-educated North American Negroes like Angela Davis, who were caught up in the romance of Third World revolution and terrified of being prejudiced against their own kind. Rings of guilt were run through their noses, and they were pulled along in their iron suits by lawbreakers who told them that they were incapable of speaking for the people or exhibiting the courage necessary to overthrow the racist, capitalist structure of the United States.

In a perfect example of ambition realized, Black Panther founder and leader Huey Newton turned the radical political front of his group into a cover for the organized extortion and murder he so admired in Mario Puzo's *The Godfather* (which he required his closest followers to read). Addicted to cocaine before his racket fell apart, Newton's death outside a crack house at the hands of a dealer working for a cocaine crew called The Black Guerrilla Family was more than fitting. Angela Davis is now a professor of alienation in the academy, and a good number of Newton's white supporters, like rock critics and record executives, have found fresher rebellious fish to fry.

The grand irony of this MTV version of street crime as outlaw radicalism is that the growing power of international organized crime, ever an amoral threat to democratic freedom, facilitates the drugs which produce so much of the blood-letting in the streets of the United States and set the tone for so much of the street crime that gives a bloody image of the United States to the world. That anarchic reign of terror has unarguably removed individual freedom from the most beleaguered communities. Yet the extremes of antisocial behavior are celebrated in the world of pop music as though they are not only street-smart antidotes to the various restrictions of bourgeois life but also noble savage critiques of both big business and the crooked racists who live in the shadow worlds where they supposedly pull the controlling strings of our government. In essence, the MTV executives and the record producers are no different than the South American drug lords who reside in palaces and on grounds that are paeans to overstatement while supplying the powders that increase the desperation and speed the decay of the slums.

Because gangster rap so haughtily claims to express an "authenticity" unblemished by so-called white society, it also plays into the hands of those already convinced of Afro-American inferiority, those who would push Negroes into an iron suit of specious genetic theories and class-oriented ideas about the inevitability of lower-class failure. These guardians who are so exasperated by the failures of social programs in the United States can now stand at the gates and assert, one way or another,

> We didn't have to say that you were incorrigibly outside the fundamental morality and the methods of honest upward mobility in our democracy. We didn't have to say that your actions express

an unrelenting hatred of the civilization that drives and sustains the United States. You did.

That is why we cannot be intimidated by resentment from the bottom to the top, the top to the bottom. The corruptions of protest shouldn't make it impossible for us to assert the sophistication necessary to utilize the double-edged sword of accurate assessment. Nor should we be bullied by those who claim that we can only protect our civilization by excluding those at the bottom.

History teaches us — over and over and over — that no community, young or old, is immune to the hopped-up irrationalities of scapegoating. We can never forget that almost all totalitarian orders begin as youth movements disgusted by almost everything in the established order and impatient with the slow, difficult processes of actual human development within the context of individual liberty under the rule of law. It can never be said too often that the "temples of light," the pageantry, and the mindless incantation of Adolf Hitler made him the first rock star and perhaps the first gangster rapper as well. Appeals to resentment, alienation, separatist "authenticity," and tribal paranoia always seek to manipulate the anti-intellectual adolescent within all of us, regardless of our age. Such appeals all produce old and rusty or new and polished lines of iron suits, whether they come from the top or the bottom, the bottom or the top.

America's Boiling Gumbo Pot

We can most effectively move in the direction of melting down the iron suits of history by celebrating the fundamental vitality of one charismatic fact: Our many miscegenations don't imprison us in any of the many varieties of resentment and paranoia if we truly understand them. They supply our democratic liberation through the enrichments of identity. We can no longer afford to traffic in simpleminded and culturally inaccurate terms like "black" and "white" if they are meant to convey anything more than loose descriptions of skin tone. We are the results of every human possibility that has touched us, no matter its point of origin. As people of the Americas, we rise up from a gumbo in which, by now, it is sometimes very difficult to tell one ingredient from another. All those ingredients, however, give a more delectable taste to the brew.

Here are but a few of the many luminous examples. Unlike the mutations and unintentional alliances of bad faith, they provide us with democratic clarity.

No amount of anti-Hispanic propaganda stopped the emergence of the Latin lover as a symbol of magnetism and elegance; no amount of hostility toward the United States halted the influence of North American dance bands on South American music nor the appeal of Afro-Hispanic rhythms to North American musicians and dancers; none of the wars with Mexico limited the effect of Mexican vaqueros on the American cowboy; anti-Semitism was no more than a sieve through which the Jewish stream of contributions to film, comedy, music, politics, science, law, and literature gushed; the rough and tumble chicanery of United States' companies in Latin countries didn't keep American movies and writers from having significant impact on South American literature and film; Gabriel Garcia Marquez's friendship with Fidel Castro put no limits on the way in which his appropriation and personalizing of William Faulkner into "magic realism" came North and touched writers from the Atlantic to the Pacific coasts; the hysteria over the threat of Asian immigration was overwhelmed by the love of Chinese food, sushi, Asian philosophy, and martial arts; neither racism nor segregation checked the influence of Negroes throughout the Americas.

The richest music of the United States is jazz, itself a miscegenated mixture of elements African, European, and Hispanic. Jazz improvisation brought together a sensitivity to mutual invention within a form that fused Western harmony and thematic variation with the shifting, incantatory rhythms derived from Africa. Jazz achieves its power not through anarchy but through that creative cooperation in which the responsible quality of individual improvisation elevates the communicative power and the order of the whole. It calls for a gathering, not a scattering.

Jelly Roll Morton, himself a New Orleans Creole, the first great jazz composer and its first theorist, said that jazz music wasn't complete without "the Spanish Tinge." Louis Armstrong, who was also born in New Orleans and appears as a giant of international cultural innovation in a number of novels and short stories written south of the border of the United States, spoke through his horn most eloquently of our rich mutations of identity and culture in the Americas when he played the introduction to "The St. Louis Blues" in its tango rhythm. He lifted up his horn as he rose from the boiling gumbo pot of the Western Hemisphere like a brown Poseidon of melody. Armstrong was then calling up the heroic, Afro-American lyricism of hope swelling out beyond deep recognition of tragedy and was also enriching our ambivalent sense of adult romance through the beat of that matchless dance in which all of the complexities of courtship and romantic failure seem to have located themselves in the Argentinian steps of endless ballroom couples so expressive of passionate nuances they seem forever mythic. The transcending power of such combinations are symbolic of the affirmative, miscegenated heat necessary to melt down the iron suits of history.

VICTORY IS ASSURED!

Chapter 14

Pocho Pioneer

Richard Rodriguez

It is appropriate that I come to this distinguished encuentro as something of a naysayer. It is appropriate, though ironic, that I sound a sour note in the midst of all your talk about "a new moment in the Americas." As a child, I grew up in blond California where everyone was optimistic about losing weight and changing the color of her hair and becoming someone new. Only my Mexican father was dour and sour in California — always reminding me how tragic life was, how nothing changes, reminding me that everything would come to nothing under a cloudless sky.

Mexicans speak of "el fatalismo del Indio" — the sadness at the heart of Latin America. As a child, when I looked South, I shuddered at the Latin sensibility. I turned away from it, spent my childhood running toward Doris Day and Walt Disney.

You cannot imagine the irony with which I regard this meeting. My Latin American colleagues have travelled several thousand miles north to speak about the new democratic spirit in their countries, the new spirit of individualism. We of the north, by contrast, have become a dark people. We do not vote. We have lost our optimism. We are besotted with individualism and we have grown lonely. We, in California, now sound very much like my Mexican father.

I end up a "pocho" in the United States, reflecting on the tragic nature of life.

Clearly, I am a freak of history. I carry this Indian face; I have a Spanish surname; my first name is Richard (*Ree-cherd*, Mexico calls me). The great Octavio Paz, in *The Labyrinth of Solitude,* has a chapter concerned with the "pachuco" — the teenaged gangster in Los Angeles. For Paz the gang kids of California represent the confusion within the Mexican American — caught between two cultures. The child does not know where he belongs. The child has lost his address. The child no longer belongs to Mexico, neither does he

This is Richard Rodriguez's revised version of the speech he delivered at "A New Moment in the Americas," on November 12, 1994.

fit into the United States. The Mexican American is a tragic figure, a pathetic one. Señor Paz is right about Mexican Americans, but he is also arrogant and wrong about us.

Consider these the reflections of a pocho...

You know, we sit here in this elegant room, talking about the new moment in the Americas as though the moment has just happened, today — November 12, 1994. We act as though we are the witnesses of its happening. In fact, the so-called moment, the discovery of the Americas by Americans, has been going on for nearly a century. But the discovery has been mainly by peasants. They were the first Americans who trespassed American borders.

I speak of the hundreds of thousands of migrant workers who have been coming to the United States since the turn of the century. The two largest groups: Puerto Ricans and Mexicans. Back and forth they went, across borders, time zones, languages, faiths. Between Puerto Rico and New York, between Los Angeles and Mexico.

The Puerto Ricans found themselves, at the end of the nineteenth century, suddenly part of the United States. The Mexicans found themselves in places like Arizona and California, which used to be part of Mexico. The Mexicans and Puerto Ricans were like no other immigrant group the United States had ever seen. There was something wrong with us.

And yet I would like to argue that we were the first Americans — Americans, that is, in the sense we are talking today. The peasants of Puerto Rico and Mexico were the first people who saw the hemisphere whole.

Oh, there is President Salinas de Gortari today with his Harvard degrees, as there are the new "technocrats" of Latin America with their Ivy League degrees. Business executives and government officials in the United States sigh with relief at meeting this new class of Latin Americans.

"At last, Señor Salinas, we understand you. You speak our language. You are our kind of Mexican. Let's talk business."

Do not listen to the flattery of the United States, Señor Salinas. I am sorry to have to tell you that you have been preceded North to the United States by several decades, by millions of peasants.

Mexican Americans, Puerto Ricans — we were a puzzle to the United States. We were people from the South in the east-west country. (The United States has written its history across the page, east to west. The United States saw its manifest destiny unfolding in the western migration.) Land was the crucial metaphor for possibility in the United States' scheme of things. As long as there was land, there was possibility. As long as you could move West, you had a future. As long as you could leave Maryland for Nebraska, then you could change the color of your hair, change your religion. As long as you could leave Kansas for Nevada, you could drop your father's name or shorten it. You could drop the embarrassing "ini" or "izzi" or "stein." You could become someone other than your father.

I am going to California to become Tab Hunter. Yes, I like that name. Me llamo Tab Hunter.

The crisis in California today is due to the fact that the United States has run out of land. The metaphor of the west has been exhausted. The end had been decades in coming. As early as the 1860s, there were premonitions of finitude in California. In the 1860s, when California was newly U.S. territory, environmentalists reached the coast with a sense of dread. John Muir stood at the beach in the 1860s and announced to the United States that he had come to the edge of possibility: America is a finite idea. We have to start saving America. We have to start saving the land. Conserving America. The message went back — west to east — back to the crowded brick cities of the East Coast.

I grew up in the 1950s when California was filling with people from Nebraska and Minnesota. People arrived from Brooklyn, or they came from Chicago. They came for a softer winter. They came to recreate themselves.

But shortly we ran out of land. Los Angeles got too crowded and needed to reinvent itself as Orange County. Then Orange County got too crowded and had to reinvent itself as north county San Diego. Then north county San Diego got too crowded. Now Californians are moving into the desert. We don't have enough room any more, we say.

Suddenly foreign immigrants are coming. They are pouring into California from the South. ("We are sorry to intrude, señor, we are looking for work.") They come from Latin America, talking of California as "el Norte," not the West Coast. El Norte is wide open. The West Coast is a finite idea. *Whose map is correct?*

There are planes landing in Los Angeles today, planes from Thailand, from Hong Kong, planes from Seoul and from Taiwan. People getting off the planes say about California, "This is where the United States begins." Those of us in the United States who believe in the western route to California say, "No, no. California is where the United States comes to an end." *Whose myth is true?*

People in the United States used to say, "Go West, young man." We meant, go West toward possibility. Now that we have hit against the wall of the coastline, we start talking about going East. "Go East, young man!"

"I'm leaving California; I'm going to Nebraska."

"I'm leaving California; I'm going to Colorado."

And, for the first time, today Californians speak of the North and the South. Not because we want to. Not because we are accustomed to looking North and South. It's only because the West is a finite idea.

"I'm going to get a condominium in Baja California. You know, there are condos throughout Baja where everyone speaks English. We're going to make Baja our national park."

Or, "I'm leaving California for Canada. I'm going to Vancouver. There are too may ethnics in California. I'm going to Canada where the air is cleaner."

Go North, young man.

Puerto Ricans, Mexicans — early in this century we were a people from the South in an east-west country. We were people of mixed blood in a black and white country. America's great scar, its deep tear, has always been the black and white division. Puerto Ricans and Mexicans tended to be of mixed race. Hard, therefore, for the United States to classify or even see.

For the last thirty years in the United States, Hispanics have impersonated a race. We have convinced bureaucrats in Washington — bureaucrats who knew nothing about us and cared less — that we constituted a racial group. It was essential, if the United States were ever to recognize us, that we be a racial group, people subject to "racial discrimination."

The only trouble is, Hispanics do not constitute a racial group. But what does the United States care? There we are in the ponderous morning pages of *The New York Times*, listed on a survey alongside black, white, Asian.

Puerto Ricans, Mexicans — we were Catholics in a Protestant country. And millions of us were Indians in a country that imagined the Indian to be dead. Today, Los Angeles is the largest Indian city in the United States. All around the city, you can see Toltecs and Aztecs and Mayans. But the filmmakers of Hollywood persist in making movies about the dead Indian. For seven dollars, you can see cowboys kill the Indians. We are sorry about it. We feel the luxury of regret from our swivel seats.

On the other hand, I remember a chic dinner party in Mexico City. (You know, rich Mexicans can be very polite when they say cruel things. It is their charm.) One Mexican, a drink in his hand, said to me, "You are a writer? Very interesting. Your work has been translated in Mexico?"

I replied, "Well, not much."

He said, "Well, we Mexicans are not going to know what to make of you as a writer." He said, "We're not accustomed to writers who look like you."

Seriously, let me apologize. I must *apologize* for not being able to speak to many of you in your own language. I suffer from this strange disability. I can understand spoken Spanish, can read it. But I can't speak Spanish with ease. I walk through Latin American cities like a sleepwalker, comprehending everything but unable to join the conversation.

How shall I explain my disability? Elena Castedo, in her wonderful essay on the United States, suggested that we in the United States are afraid of foreign languages. That is true, but not quite right. Better to say that we are obsessed with foreign languages. Most of us in this country are one or two generations from a grandparent who scolded us for losing her language. There is an enormous guilt in the American soul.

I want you to know that I have been haunted by Spanish for most of my life. I understand your jokes and your asides. I hear your whisperings. I smile feebly in response. I feel so guilty about not being able to join you. It is because I have taken this new lover, American English, this blond lover of mine has taken my breath away.

Hispanics in the United States turn into fools. We argue among ourselves, criticize one another, mock one another for becoming too much the gringo. We criticize each other for speaking too much Spanish or not enough Spanish. We demand that our politicians provide us with bilingual voting ballots, but we do not bother to vote. We are, as Señor Paz observed decades ago, freaks of history.

I have heard Mexicans of the middle class say to their children, when their children head for the United States to go to college, "Stay away from those Chicanos, whatever you do. Stay away from them because they're crazy. They think of themselves as 'minorities.'"

We are Mexico's Mexicans. Everything Mexico loathes about herself she hates in us. We lost our culture to a larger power. Mexico lost her tongue to Cortés. For us Cortés is Uncle Sam. If I go back to Mexico, Mexico comes closer to me, breathes in my ear. "Hijito, háblame en español," Mexico says.

I say, "Ay, Madre, no puedo. No más un poquito."

"Un poquito. Un poquito. Tu propio idioma...!"

Then, POCHO.

Michael Novak was speaking last night about what unites the hemisphere. What unites us as Americans, he said, is our willingness to say goodbye to the motherland. We say to Europe, farewell. And there is bravery in that cry of goodbye.

The only trouble is that adiós was never part of the Mexican American or the Puerto Rican vocabulary. We didn't turn our backs on the past. We kept going back and forth, between past and future. After a few months of work in New York or Los Angeles, we would cross the border. We were commuters between centuries, between rivals. And neither country understood us.

Abuelita didn't understand us because our Spanish was so bad. On the other hand, people in the United States would wonder what was wrong with us. Why do you people need to keep going back home? (In a country that believes so much in the future our journey home was almost a subversion.) The United States said to us, "When my parents left Sweden, they didn't keep going back to Sweden. But you — you keep turning back. What's the matter with you? Are you a mama's boy?"

Pocho.

Someone said last night that the gringo had hijacked the word "American" and given it to himself with typical arrogance. I remember my aunt in Mexico City scolding me when I told her I was from America. Didn't I realize the entire hemisphere is America? Listen, my Mexican aunt told me, "People who live in the United States are norteamericanos."

Well, I think to myself — my aunt is now dead. God rest her soul — but I think to myself, I wonder what she would have thought when the great leaders — the president of Mexico, the president of the United States, the Canadian prime minister — signed the North American Free Trade Agreement. Mexico woke up one morning to realize that she's a norteamericana.

I predict that Mexico will have a nervous breakdown in ten years. She will have to check into a clinic for a long rest. She will need to determine just what exactly it means that she is, with the dread gringo, a North American.

Meanwhile, the peasants keep crossing the border. The diplomats keep signing the documents. But has anyone ever met a North American? Oh, I know. You know Mexicans. And you know Canadians. But has anyone met a North American?

I have.

Let me tell you about him, this North American. He's a Mixteco Indian who lives in the Mexican state of Oaxaca. He is trilingual. His primary language is the language of his tribe. He speaks Spanish, the language of Cortés, as a second language. Also, he has a working knowledge of U.S. English.

He knows thousands of miles of dirt roads and freeways. He commutes between two civilizations. He is preyed upon by corrupt Mexican police who want to "shake him down" because he has hidden U.S. dollars in his shoes. He is pursued as "illegal" by the U.S. border patrol. He lives in a sixteenth century village where his wife watches blond Venezuelan soap operas. There is a picture of La Virgen de Guadalupe over his bed. He works near Stockton, California, where there is no Virgin Mary but the other Madonna — the rock star.

This Mexican peasant knows two currencies. But he is as illegal on one side of the border as he is an embarrassment to his government on the other side of the line. *He* is the first North American.

People in the United States have always been wary of Mexican water. We love your beaches and your pre-Columbian ruins. But we are afraid to sing in the shower at the hotel. On the other hand, we have always trusted Canadian water. We drink gallons of it. We also assumed that Canadian water was clean.

But there is a virus in Canadian water called "multiculturalism" which is making its way into the United States' blood stream. The most interesting thing we think to say about one another now in the United States is that we are multicultural. But, of course, when people in the United States talk about multiculturalism, they mean, like the Canadians, culture to signify only race or ethnicity. In fact, culture means many other things, too.

Culture means region. What part of the world, what sky governs your life? I come from California.

Culture means age. The old man looks at the young boy with incomprehension.

Sex is culture — that great divide between the male and female, their delight and their frustration.

Religion. The United States is a Protestant country though we do not like to describe ourselves in that way.

We are a Puritan country.

A friend of mine, Pico Iyer, who writes of the confusion of cultures in the U.S. metropolis, speculates about the inevitable confusion that results when so many races, so many languages, altars, meet in modern Los Angeles. I think the more interesting dilemma for the post-modern citizen of the city is that she feels herself multicultural within herself: *How shall I reconcile the world within my own soul?*

My father remembers a Mexico that no longer exists. My father remembers a village. "Where is it, Papa? Show me where, in the state of Colima, you were a boy. Where?"

He explores the map with his finger. The city of Colima has swallowed up the village. The city has grown bloated, has larded itself over the countryside, obliterating the village.

"It is not there," he says.

We Mexican Americans end up like the British Columbians. If you go to British Columbia, you can visit houses and see the Queen of England on the wall. People use tea cozies in British Columbia. They remember an England that is nothing like the Britain of blue-haired soccer punks who beat up Pakistanis on Saturday nights. The British Columbians remember an England that exists nowhere on earth but on a faded post card.

My father remembers a Mexico that used to be a village.

A friend of mine, a European, was a hippie in northern Mexico during the 1960s. Recently my friend took his son back to Mexico to look for the villages where he was a bohemian.

My friend phoned me the other night with chagrin. He said, "Everything has changed. The little towns — no one hangs out anymore. All the Mexicans are working at the local maquiladora." And he says, "Thirty years ago, Mexicans used to walk around these small towns wearing guns. Now nobody wears guns."

I say to my friend, "If you want to see Mexicans wearing guns, go to East Los Angeles." My relatives in Mexico City, they watch ESPN. My niece in Mexico City is inordinately proud of her tee-shirt which proclaims HARD ROCK CAFE. My relatives in Mexico City have wandered away from Roman Catholicism in favor of Buddhism. My relatives in Mexico City are divorced.

At this moment, about this time in the afternoon, there are minibuses going South — Jehovah's Witnesses, Mormons. This is the great moment of conversion in the Mormon world. By the end of the century, half of the world's Mormon population will be Spanish-speaking, at which time what will we think of Salt Lake City? And of course, here come the evangelical Christians. They are converting Latin America. The great soul of Latin America is turning toward the Easter promise of Protestantism. "You are redeemed! You can change! You can become a new man! You can put away the old ways, become someone new, praise the Lord! Hallelujah!"

A Lutheran pastor I know in San Francisco works with immigrants from Central America. He often notices that, without even asking, without even thinking too much about it, the immigrants convert to Protestantism as they

settle in the United States. The conversion becomes part of their Americanization. They seem to sense that in becoming Americans, they should also
become Protestant.

On the other hand, the other day in Tijuana, Mexico, I met three boys
from an evangelical church called Victory Outreach. (Victory Outreach works
with kids who suffer from serious drug problems.) The kids said they are
coming to the United States this year — 502 years after Columbus — they are
coming to the United States to convert us back to our Protestant roots. The
youngest one said, "Those Americans are so sad."

Someone once asked Chou En-lai, the Chinese prime minister, what he
thought of the French Revolution. Chou En-lai gave a wonderful Chinese
response. He said, "It's too early to tell."

I think it may be too early to tell what the story of Columbus means.
The latest chapter of the Columbus story might be taking place right now, as
the Hispanic evangelicals head north. Who says ideas don't travel in both
directions?

The kids on the line tonight in Tijuana, if you ask them why they are
coming to the United States of America, will not say anything about Thomas
Jefferson or notions of democracy. They have not heard about Thomas Paine
or the *Federalist Papers*. They have only heard that there is a job in Glendale,
California, at a dry cleaners.

They are going back to Mexico in a few months, they insist. They are
only going to the United States for the dollars. They don't want to be gringos.
They don't want anything to do with the United States, except for the dollars.

But then a few months will pass, and they will not go back to Latin
America. What will happen, of course, to their surprise, is that the job in
Glendale will make them part of the United States. (Work in the United States
is our primary source of identity.)

People in this country, when they meet one another, do not ask about
family or where you come from. The first thing people in the U.S. ask each
other at cocktail parties is what the other does for a living.

The hemisphere, the story of the hemisphere, began with a little joke
about maps and the fact that Columbus, our papasito, our father, got it all
wrong. He imagined he was in some part of the world where there were
Indians. He thought he had come to India.

We laugh today because papi didn't know where he was. But I'm not
sure we know where we are, either. We are only beginning to look at the
map. We are only beginning to wonder what the map of the hemisphere
means.

The story of the Americas began with a cartographer's whimsy in the
Renaissance: *Is the world flat?* And to the delight of the mapmaker, the
explorer set out on the sea to discover the great human possibility of
roundness.

Mexican Americans, Puerto Ricans — we ended up in the United States
city. We are people from the village. We ended up in the city. We ended up

with a bad knowledge of English, a failing knowledge of Spanish. Yet we were remarkable people. We travelled many thousands of miles, some of us on foot. We ended up cooking for the United States or making beds or gardening. We have become the nannies of North America. We take care of the blond children of Beverly Hills and Park Avenue — these children will become the next generation of Hispanics. We have subverted, invaded, the wealthiest homes in America.

The kids in East LA, the kids that Octavio Paz was talking about forty years ago, the pachucos have turned murderous against one another. Several months ago I was talking to some gang kids in Los Angeles about New York. The photographer working with me was from New York. I asked one of the gang kids, "Would you like to see New York some day?"

The littlest one piped in response, "Not me, man."

I said, "Why not? Don't you want to see where Joe, the photographer, comes from?"

"Not me, man! I'm Mexican. I belong here."

Here? This boy lives within four blocks. If he goes a fifth block he's going to get his head blown off because he doesn't use the right sign language or he is wearing the wrong color today. This Mexican kid couldn't even find his way to the beaches of Los Angeles.

The odd thing, the tragic irony, is that many times our fathers and grandfathers who were so brave, who travelled so many thousands of miles, trespassed borders, end up with grandchildren who become Chicanos, timid children who believe that culture is some little thing put in a box, held within four blocks.

One of the things that Mexico had never acknowledged about my father, I insist that you today at least entertain — the possibility that my father and others like him were the great revolutionaries of Mexico. They, not Pancho Villa, not Zapata, were heralds of the modern age. They went back to Mexico and changed Mexico forever. The man who worked in Chicago in the 1920s returned one night to his village in Michoacán. The village gathered around him — this is a true story — and the village asked, "What is it like up there in Chicago?"

The man said, "It's okay."

That rumor of "okay" spread across Michoacán, down to Jalisco, across Jalisco into Oaxaca, from village to village to village.

There are now remote villages in Latin America that have become the most international places in the world. Tiny Peruvian villages know when they are picking pears in the Yakima Valley in the state of Washington.

We talk about the new moment in the Americas. The moment has been going on for decades. People have been travelling back and forth.

I am the son of a prophet. I am a fool. I am a victim of history. I am confused. I do not know whether I am coming or going. I speak bad Spanish. And yet, I will tell you this: to grow up Hispanic in the United States is to know more Guatemalans than if I grew up in Mexico. Because I live in California, I know more Brazilians than I would know if I lived in Peru. Because I live in California, it is routine for me to know Nicaraguans and Salvadorans and Cubans — as routine as meeting Chinese or Greeks.

People in California talk about the "illegals." But there was always an illegality to immigration. It was a rude act, the leaving of home. It was a violation of custom, an insult to the village. A youthful act of defiance. I know a man from El Salvador who has not talked to his father since the day he left his father's village. (It is a sin against family to leave home.) Immigrants must always be illegal. Immigrants are always criminals. They trespass borders and horrify their grandmothers.

But they are also our civilization's prophets. They, long before the rest of us, long before this room, long before this conference was ever imagined, they saw the hemisphere whole.